Buying Your First Home

Ricki Eichler McCallum

Buying Your First Home

A Step-by-Step Guide from Dreams to Reality

Ricki Eichler McCallum

Copyright © Ricki Eichler McCallum

Original Edition
December 5, 2020
Revised Edition March 1, 2025
All Rights Reserved

No part of this book may be reproduced or transmitted in any form or by any means; electronic or mechanical including photocopying, recording, or by any information storage and retrieval system without permission in writing from the Author.

The author and publisher have made every effort to ensure the information in this book is accurate as of press time. The author and publisher hereby disclaim and do not assume liability for any loss, injury, damage, or disruption caused by errors or omissions, regardless of whether any errors or omissions result from negligence, accident, or any other cause. Readers are encouraged to verify any information contained in this book prior to taking any action on the information.

CastNet Press

www.castnetpress.com

ISBN-13: 9798573604572

Printed in the United States of America

Also by Ricki Eichler McCallum

Finally A Broker!
Open Your Own Real Estate Office

Downsizing Homes
What You Need To Know

PANDEMIC Real Estate
Buyers, Sellers, and Realtors®

Dedication

To our Founding Fathers, who knew
Private Property Rights
given to average Americans would be the catalyst
for growing a great country.

PREFACE

Owning your own home is very important. It develops stability in a family, helps build wealth, and adds to the enjoyment of one's life. As a Mother and Grandmother, my advice is to get started as soon as possible. As a Realtor®, my advice is the same. As an Author, my desire is to inform and help first-time home buyers.

I have been a real estate broker for over 40 years and have helped many first-time home buyers realize their dreams. Working with first-time home buyers is a joy. The excitement they share, and the optimism is thrilling. Helping people buy their first home is a memorable adventure for buyers and agents alike. This book will take you through the process and help you understand the benefits of home ownership.

Writing this book was indeed, **a labor of love**. Things I might have forgotten to tell my children and grandchildren are all written here. So, if you are my family, my friend, my past client, or one of my readers, this book is for you.

It is written for your benefit. It contains a wealth of information that will help you buy your first home and many more homes in the future. Educate yourself about real estate and your life will be enriched.

The book is broken into two sections. The first is an overview of the process from your dreams to reality. The team you assemble to help you meet your goals. The second section goes into more detail about various aspects of the transaction including the contract form, termination options, inspections, appraisals, and closing.

In Chapter 16, there are examples of real-life experiences of first-time home buyers. You may relate to some of my past clients. Working with first-time home buyers was always a joy. The excitement they shared with me, and the gratitude made the hardest transactions seem easy. I did not use their real names but they were my clients.

My thanks to Tony Stevenson for sharing input concerning loan applications and processes. Tony Stevenson is the kind of professional loan originator that rarely comes along. I am privileged to know him and to have worked with him for my clients' sake.

My thanks to all my former clients that allowed me the honor of representing them in transactions. The journey was not always easy, but it was always rewarding, knowing the great people that became my clients and friends.

My thanks to my wonderful husband who endured the writing, and helped proof this book. Thank you for your love, your effort and time to make this dream a reality.

Ricki Eichler McCallum,

Author, Real Estate Broker, Realtor®,

ABR, GRI, e-Pro, TAHS

Table of Contents

Section One

Chapter 1	Step 1, Defining The Dream	5
Chapter 2	What the Dream Looks Like	11
Chapter 3	Step 2, The Plan	22
Chapter 4	Step 3, Agent Representation	32
Chapter 5	Finding the Right Agent	40
Chapter 6	Step 4, Reality Begins with Home Search	48

Section Two

Chapter 7	Loans and Your Originator	63
Chapter 8	The Contract Form	72
Chapter 9	Termination Option and Inspections	83
Chapter 10	The Appraisal	89

Chapter 11	Taxes and Insurance	96
Chapter 12	Home Warranties	103
Chapter 13	Title Company and Closing	107
Chapter 14	Moving	113
Chapter 15	Maintenance and Landscaping	118
Chapter 16	Real Life Experiences of First-time Home Buyers	126

Glossary of Terms   140

Author Notes

Section One

Introduction

George and Julie married one year ago. They dated two years before getting married, and everyone says they are the perfect couple. George, a policeman works in the mid-sized city where they reside. Julie works for a family practice doctor as a receptionist. They make a comfortable living and have enough money to dine out on the weekends and go to an occasional ball game or concert.

Their apartment lease is almost ready to renew, and the rent is going up $200 per month. They both want to own their own home, but they do not know how to begin or who to talk to.

George's mom raised him alone, as his dad died while serving in the Armed Forces. His mom always rented an apartment. George had no other siblings, and his mom never remarried. He learned nothing about home ownership since the apartment complex provided maintenance, so his mom never worried about fixing anything that broke. Owning a home and maintaining it properly will be all new to George.

As a child, Julie and her parents lived in the same home her grandparents owned for decades. When they passed away, Julie's parents inherited the home and they still live there today. Julie has no knowledge of buying real property and it scares her because of the unknown.

George and Julie want to have children in a few years, and raise them in a neighborhood where they'll have playmates. A nearby park with a playground would be ideal. They can imagine their future home with all the amenities they need and want. They talk about it a lot and hope their dreams will come true.

George wants a big garage and a place to store his camping gear and flat-bottom boat. Julie wants a large kitchen, enormous clothes closet, and a separate utility room with a new washer and dryer. These items are not in their apartment, so spending another year or two there seems like the wrong idea, if they can buy a home now.

George and Julie are the perfect example of first-time homebuyers. Are you a first-time homebuyer? Do you want to buy but don't know how, or where to begin? With this book, you will learn the process of buying your first home.

It is easier than people think. Knowing the processes ahead of time will provide the confidence for doing it right. Chapters on credit, loans, how to choose the right house, and agent to represent you, will be addressed. Included is information about title policies, purchase offers, termination options, contract deadlines, closing costs, inspections, maintaining your home, warranties and much more.

Home Ownership

is the

American Dream

Chapter 1

Step 1, Defining The Dream

Dreams are good for everyone. Do not be afraid to dream and dream big! Dreams are like wishes, and goals are like plans. Put them in the right order with action, and they become reality. So it is, with buying your first home.

Every home purchase begins with a dream. You want to own your home. You need more space or amenities like a bigger kitchen, a garage, or a fenced backyard. **Wants and needs** are the motivation in home buying.

Wants are things that would be nice to have. Needs are something you must have. Start with a list of wants and needs. Take the time to dream. You can afford to dream big on paper. Write down all those wants and needs. Put them in separate columns so you will know which ones are expendable and which ones are not if you must delete some.

If you are married or buying a home with a partner, each of you should write a separate list. Then, you can sit down and look at one another's lists and begin to eliminate the things you don't have to have. Focus on the needs of each person. The needs must be met or one partner will be happy and the other will never feel satisfied.

Discuss each item on your lists, so each person understands why the item is there and how important it is to the one who wants or needs it. Slowly eliminate items and combine them into one list. This may take some time. Make a list that is good for both of you. If you have children, you should consider their wants and needs as well. The parents will have the last say in any decision but the child's perspective should be considered. Happy families have happy homes.

Now, let's consider the wants and needs of a single home buyer. More and more single people are buying homes today. No matter what your lifestyle is, owning your home can bring satisfaction.

Why pay rent when you can own? That's a lot of money going to a landlord. When buying a home, you are actually saving a portion of the money you would pay as a rental payment or house payment, if you own your home. The increase in equity every month soon amounts to quite a bit of increased net worth. The sooner you buy, the more equity you stand to receive when you are ready to sell.

Your first home purchase may be very scary but this book will help to relieve some of the tension associated with buying a home, especially a first home. You may be in your early adulthood, or you may be middle-aged. Some people buy their first home in retirement years. It does not matter how old you are. The tension and uncertainty will always be there. Press on. It is worth the trouble to live in your own home. To have total control of your property, to say this is mine, is a feeling like none other.

I remember the day I closed on my first home. I was very young and the excitement was so great, I didn't even feel afraid. I felt more afraid of not buying. I wanted to know when I hung my clothes in the closet, that closet was mine. When I turned on the water tap, that faucet handle belonged to me. I could lock the front door and the space inside my home was all mine. It was a sanctuary. I controlled the space, the air, the floors, the walls, the appliances, it was mine!

It was a marvelous feeling! I will never forget the freedom I had in my first home.

I had lived in a duplex before I bought my first home. The landlord, an old man that lived across the street, was watering the flowers in my yard every morning. He would be out there early every day. One day, I caught him trying to look into my windows. I yelled at him, and he walked away mumbling to himself. I immediately started looking for a place of my own.

A week later, I came home and found him in my house. I again, yelled at him and told him to leave and never to come inside my place again when I was gone. This was many years ago, and today, I would have called the police. Back then, I was young and I did not know what to do. He owned my residence and laws were different then. I moved out shortly and into my own home.

Knowing I was the only one with a key to my house, gave me such a peaceful feeling. I could sleep at night and not be afraid, and I could open the curtains in the daytime and not have someone watering flowers in my yard. This place belonged to me and I controlled everything about it. It was freedom and it was peace and security.

I believe everyone that can, should own their home. I have been in the real estate business for forty years and sold thousands of houses to clients and many were first time homebuyers. I will explain in this book all the necessary steps you need to take to make your first home purchase a reality.

Chapters 1 and 2, **THE DREAM.** You must have a dream, if you want it to come true.

Chapter 3, you must have **THE PLAN,** how to get a mortgage and get to where you want to be.

Chapter 4 and 5, Dreams and Plans are nothing without **THE ACTION.** Finding the right agent and getting buyer representation.

Chapter 6, after all this work, you now have **THE REALITY.** Time for your home search, the fun part.

I will explain the shopping process for a home, how to choose the right agent, how to obtain financing, how to get inspections, what title policies are and why you need one. I will share tips with you, to make sure you get the most for your money. This book will even touch on decorating and landscaping.

Prepare yourself, before you go shopping for a home. Reading this book, **'Buying Your First Home'** can be the beginning of the process. So, get reading and begin to make your dreams come true.

Chapter 2

What the Dream Looks Like

Your dream is now written on paper. You and your spouse, or partner have thoroughly discussed what your wants and needs are. You have both compromised and settled on many of your wants and needs but the needs always win out. However, there are still a few wants included in your dream list.

Let's look at the list in more detail. We will start with **bedrooms**. This is the easiest part. You know how many bedrooms you must have. This depends on how large your family is, or how large you plan for it to become, and how many extra rooms you might want to convert into an office, study or hobby room. What you want and what you can live with are two different things. Look at the reality, but also look at possibilities. Do not get these two confused. When money is tight, people dream about changing a property in the future. Sometimes, that is possible. If the home is arranged properly, you might add a bedroom at a later date. Most of the time, however, it is better to just buy an upgrade than try to change a floorplan.

In my real estate business, I have seen many homes with added bedrooms. Many times, the construction was poor and the bedroom did not fit the original floorplan. Sometimes, there was no access to the bedroom unless you walked into it from another bedroom. This is called functional obsolescence. It often takes value from the property rather than adding value. So, be careful if you plan on adding onto your home in the future. You need to know what you are doing. Consult professionals before making major changes in the first home you buy. Consider, the first home a stepping stone to another home in the future if your family outgrows it.

Next, we will focus on the **number of baths**. Once again, bathrooms are one of the most important rooms in the house. If you have children, or parents living with you, you will need to consider at least two bathrooms if not more. A half bath has a sink and a toilet. A three quarters bath has the sink or vanity, the toilet and a shower. A full bath has vanity, toilet, and a tub, often with a shower.

An extra half bath works for lots of people, a three quarters bath for even more. If you have children, you will need a tub. So, don't buy a home without a tub in at least one of the bathrooms. Even seniors without children living at home, usually want a tub in the home they buy. When you get ready to sell your first home, you want it to appeal to as many people as possible. So, the time to think about re-selling your first home is **before** you buy it.

Kitchens and utility rooms are also important rooms. The size, the shape and location of these rooms are important as you will see once you start looking at homes. I love to cook, so a big kitchen is important to me. If you are just starting out, you probably will not have as many kitchen appliances, dishes, pots and pans as you will accumulate over a long period of time. A smaller kitchen may be what you need.

Utility rooms are very nice to have with extra cabinets and a utility sink. This may be something that is a must for you but for others a hall closet that contains the washer and dryer is all that is needed. Having a separate room means some of the square footage of the home is used for a utility room rather than more living space. Home prices are built around square footage. If you need to get as much for your money as you can, a utility closet may save some money instead of investing your square footage in a separate utility room. Your needs will dictate which is best.

Living rooms and living areas are the most used rooms in the house. The family meets here, guests are entertained here, and it is the room that defines the rest of the house. One living space may be sufficient, or you may need two, depending on the size of your family and your lifestyle.

Dining areas are often attached to kitchens or living rooms. Your preferences will determine what is a need and what is just a want.

Garages and backyards offer the most flexibility in your home search but are important to the enjoyment of your new home. A garage or storage building can be excluded if there is room to construct one at a later date. The backyard needs to be large enough to accommodate future projects like patios, pools, play equipment and outdoor kitchens. A well-designed backyard adds enjoyment and improves living space for family and friends. Parties, bar-be-que's, even meetings can be held in backyards when indoor space is limited. The warmer the climate, the more you will use outdoor facilities.

*****

The dream will include a price or monthly payment in your budget range. You can dream all day long but to make it a reality, you must focus on the price. We will break down how monthly payments are figured in this chapter. You will learn what amortization is and how it is figured. Most people can afford a house payment about the size of their current rental payment. So, start with that. If you are currently paying $1,000, 1,500, 2,000 or 3,000 per month, begin your real estate search with homes in the price range that would coordinate with a similar monthly house payment. Here's how to figure your price range.

To determine what price range of homes you need to look for, find an amortization calculator tool on Google. Bankrate.com also sponsors one that is great. It will figure loans for homes or other things. I like www.amortization-calc.com. You can print a complete amortization schedule here that will show you how much principal is paid each month. It also shows how much of your house payment is going toward interest. Each month the interest is less and the principal paid is more. This can be motivating to pay more than one principal payment each month because it could lessen the amount of interest you will pay over the term of the loan. Zillow.com also has an amortization calculator tool that is very easy to use.

An amortization schedule will figure how much your principal and interest payment is for a particular price home at a certain interest rate for a certain period of time on a monthly basis.

Let's take $200,000 for an example, with a 30-year loan at 4 % interest rate. The payment will be $995 per month **plus taxes and insurance** which **are not** figured on amortization schedules.

Taxes and insurance vary from location to location and we will discuss them fully in a proceeding chapter. For this example, we will add 400 dollars, as this is a median range. This would make your house payment to be about $1,400 per month.

If you are paying rent at the rate of $1,500 per month and not getting anything for it, doesn't it make sense to buy a home and save some of that money in the form of home equity? Also, having a home of your own adds comfort and security.

When interest rates are low, you can afford a bigger loan. Check out the website www.Bankrate.com . It compares today's mortgage rates at various banks, saving you lots of research time. This website is full of information you may need. At the top of the page, it shows you how much down payment you need for a particular home price. You can change the prices, and you can change the term of the loan (the years you will pay). It tells you what your credit score needs to be as well. It is a very helpful website; one you can use over and over again.

I have mentioned several words thus far that you may not be familiar with. For better understanding, let's define some of the terms we will be using.

(For a more complete glossary of terms, go to the back of the book.)

Amortization is making planned, incremental payments of principal and interest on a loan until it is fully paid.

Interest is an amount of money paid over the amount borrowed. It is figured as a percentage. In 2020, most mortgage rates were between 3% and 4%. They can change quickly with the market. They did and in 2025 they range between 6-7%. *When I was a young adult, I acquired some property and built a home with 19.5% interest.* That is a lot different from today's rates. Now, is a good time to buy because interest rates are low. Inflation causes rates to rise.

Principal is the amount borrowed, the price of your home minus the down payment. It is divided into monthly payments. It is amortized with the interest payment to find the monthly amount due.

Taxes are property taxes you must pay based on the assessed value of your property and any improvements to the land (basically your home, garage, and out buildings). You will pay taxes to the city, the county, the school district, the township, hospital district, maybe water district, and other entities in your area. It will generally be billed to you in one statement once or twice a year.

Insurance is homeowner's insurance which will insure your home against damage caused by various things such as fire and wind damage. Included in homeowner's insurance is insurance for contents, your personal belongings. You may need flood insurance or windstorm insurance as well. We will discuss this thoroughly in chapter 11.

Escrow account is an account held by the mortgage company for you. The account is set up at closing, with money paid by you, for taxes and insurance when they become due and payable. The mortgage company will pay these costs automatically every year.

PITI is a portion of your monthly house payment that goes for each of these: **Principal, Interest, Taxes, and Insurance**. Together these are called **PITI**.

Title policy is an insurance policy a title company issues to insure the title is good and has no clouds on the title. A cloud is anything that keeps the title company from guaranteeing the title is clear of liens or claims of ownership. Everyone should get a title policy or abstract when they purchase property. A title policy is always good and you should keep it even after you sell the property. In case there is ever a dispute about ownership, it has a monetary value to you if you are involved in a lawsuit to prove ownership.

Abstract of title is a collection of documents showing legal transactions concerning the subject property. It may go back to the beginning of the country. *I had a piece of property in Texas once, that the abstract showed the land being given to the family of a man killed at the Alamo.* An abstract will not guarantee the title is good. It just shows the lists of transactions that have occurred. Sometimes, the list may be missing transactions which could put a cloud on the title. In this case, the title policy which is an insurance policy, will protect the new buyer from a lawsuit that could arise from a previous owner's family that claims ownership in your property.

Now, don't be discouraged if all of this sounds like too much to learn. It is not. These are words, definitions you will use many times in life not just in buying a home.

If you get lost in any of my explanations, you can come back here or go to the back of the book and look up the meaning of the word again. I want you to understand. I want this book to really help you buy your first home. Read it and read it again. Use it as a reference book. If you need more help, go to my website www.castnetpress.com and email me. I will be happy to answer your questions.

Chapter 3

Step 2, The Plan

The next step after the dreaming is the planning. Now that you have the dream cemented in your mind and written on paper, you can begin to plan. The Plan, **Step 2** begins with knowing how much you can afford monthly. You have now used the amortization guides to <u>find your price range</u>.

<u>Your credit score is next.</u> It is a numeric value derived from your credit and payment history which you will find in your credit report. It gives the reviewer an idea of the probability of repayment on a future loan.

www.annualcreditreport.com offers a <u>free credit report</u> to everyone once a year.

www.experian.com offers your <u>credit score</u> for free.

Other reporting agencies will charge you but you can get your report as often as you like without it affecting your credit. The higher the credit score, the lower your interest rate will be when you get a loan. The lower the interest rate is, the less expensive your monthly house payment. *This means with good credit you can buy a more expensive house than someone with bad credit for the same monthly payment. Keeping your credit score high is worth money in your pocket.*

Mortgage companies figure credit scores a little differently than the ones you get online. They not only take the credit score into consideration but also your ability to pay back loans, the amount of time you have had credit and many other things. So, don't be surprised if the credit score they use, and the one you have been looking at from the credit score companies differs a bit. The difference is not worth worrying about, so do your best to keep your score high and check it occasionally.

Credit is important. Paying your bills on time and having credit cards that are not maxed out will improve your credit score. It takes several months to repair a bad mark on your score. So, it is important to always pay your bills on or before the due date, or you may get a bad mark on your report.

For an example, a water bill paid 3 days after the due date will drop your score several points. It will take about 3 months of paying on or before the due date on this same bill to regain those points lost. Sometimes, 5-10 points make a big difference when you are applying for a loan. So, don't let your bills go past the due date.

Banks and mortgage companies will look at any loans you have had that were delinquent, how long you have had established credit, and what kind of credit sources you have. They want to know your buying habits. How much credit you currently have available, is also a consideration. Of course, the amount of outstanding loans affects your ability to repay a mortgage loan. Your credit report holds many keys and the banker or mortgage lender will calculate all these things.

If you have some unpaid bills, even ones that went to collection agencies, showing on your credit report, try to contact the companies and get a settlement and pay back anything that is outstanding. If a disputed amount is over 7 years old, it can be removed with a letter to the company. Ask them to remove it from your report. Give them a few months to do so and if they do not, write to them again or write directly to the Credit Reporting Company.

TransUnion Dispute Removal:
800-916-8800
555 W Adams St
Chicago, IL 6066

Equifax is a little harder to resolve but here is their contact information. If you don't get anywhere with a phone call, write a letter.

Equifax Dispute Removal:
404-885-8300
1550 Peachtree St, NW
Atlanta, GA 30309

Experian may prove to be the most challenging but do not give up. Having a good credit report is essential to getting a loan and so many other things. Your credit report is very important so be ready to write a few letters.

**Experian Dispute Removal:
714-830-7000
475 Anton Blvd.
Costa Mesa, CA 92626**

Some people apply for every credit card offer that comes in the mail. I've known people that have 10-20 credit cards. Who needs that many? If you have 10 cards with a credit limit of $10,000, you will have $100,000 of credit available to you, theoretically.

If you only make minimum wage, can you see where this could be problematic for a lender considering giving you a loan to buy a house? The debt to income ratios is what a lender uses to determine your ability to repay a loan. Those 10 credit cards could be used to buy a lot of furniture on credit for the new house, then how would you pay the credit card payments and the house payment?

You would not get a loan in a scenario like this. What can you do? Call the credit card companies and cancel the cards you absolutely do not need. Do not cancel all of them. You must have a credit threshold. Bring your credit opportunities down by removing excess cards and your opportunity to get a loan just increased.

These are ways to clean up your report before you apply for a loan. Doing this before you make application for your loan, can save you the disappointment of being turned down. It will also take longer to get a new loan if you wait and do this later. So, take care of business now. Mortgage companies love clean credit reports.

"Good credit is worth more than money", a friend of mine used to say.

First part of the plan is to make sure your credit report is clean and your credit score is as high as possible.

Some young people have never established credit and do not know how to begin. If you do not have a checking account, go to your bank or credit union and set up a checking account. Use checks to pay your bills or pay them online through the checking account. You need to establish a paper trail. Getting a mortgage requires a paper trail.

After a short while, you may go see your banker and explain you need to establish credit. They may loan you a small amount of money based on your income and deposit history. If you pay this amount back in a six-to twelve-month period, you have established some credit. Take the money they give you, put it away or hold it in your account and pay it back one month at a time. It will add to your credit rating.

Many department stores issue credit cards for a small amount like $500-$1,000 to be used in their stores. Apply for a couple of these. Buy a small amount and make a few payments. The point is to make monthly payments on time. Even if you have the money to pay in full, pay it out in a few payments. This will establish your credit.

A credit rating is based on how well you pay on time over a period of time. It is also based on income and ability to repay a loan. Your good judgment is considered by how many credit cards you have, and your ability to pay them if they were maxed out. So, don't have more cards than your income can handle. Too large a credit line is worse than too small a credit line.

Second part is to find a lender. You can get a loan through a bank, credit union, or mortgage company. I recommend a mortgage company unless you have a good working relationship with a bank. I have found lots of banks are more conservative with lending and charge more for loans.

A mortgage company loan officer gets paid on commission and will bend over backwards often to get your business. They will be there to answer your questions on weekends and at night. Banks are not like that.

Find a good mortgage lender by asking friends who they used and if they got excellent service. Research the lenders online but find one that you can meet with in person. Some people rely on advice they get from the real estate agent they choose to work with to help them choose a lender. Often, the agent you work with has good working relationships with many lenders and can guide you. If you prefer to research for yourself go ahead. You can start the loan process before looking for a home. It will make your home buying experience much easier.

A lender that has been working in your area for a long time with a good reputation will be there for you in years to come. This person needs to be someone you can trust. You will be giving him or her all your personal information. You want your information to remain safe.

The process of getting a loan has many steps. The first one after you have chosen the person you want to use is to get pre-approved for your loan. This will involve giving your loan officer information about your income, and your monthly expenses. They do a simple calculation and determine what price house you should be looking for, very similar to what you have already done with the mortgage calculation tool.

The letter you get from the mortgage company will state "Based On" the information from the buyer, you would qualify for a home in the price range of blank to blank. They will fill in the blanks. You will give this pre-approval letter to your real estate agent before you begin looking for homes. This is not a letter saying you are approved for a loan because you are not. It is simply saying if you told the truth to your mortgage lending agent, you should be able to qualify for a home in the price range stated.

Later, when the home loan process continues, you will have to justify what you told the loan officer with 3 months of bank statements, w-2's, income tax returns, credit card statements, and many more documents. Getting all your records in order and having them available before you make application will save you time. You will make application for your loan now or after you find a home you want to purchase. The loan process can take a couple of months, so the sooner you begin the better.

Up to this point, you have learned a little about loans, credit scores, credit reports and more of the business side of buying a home. Don't let all this overwhelm you. Your loan officer, the person you choose to trust, will guide you through all the process. It is their job to do all the work. You must provide the information and that is a big job too.

In a later chapter, I will explain loans in more detail. It is just for your information. The more you know, the less scary it is.

Remember, how much fun it will be to come home to your own place. When you put the key in the lock and step inside, it is your own private oasis. Leave your cares at the door, you are home!

Chapter 4
Step 3, Agent Representation

With pre-approval letter from your lender in hand, **Step 3 is to find a real estate agent.** Your agent is the person that will lead you by the hand, show you properties on the market and write the contract to purchase. Your agent will represent you (I hope), your agent will negotiate offers and help you make the best buy. Agents make appointments and provide information to you about the homes they are showing you.

An agent can provide lots of information about seller's disclosures, inspections, title companies, closing procedures, loans, and so much more. Your agent is the go-between for buyer and seller or seller's agent. There are lots of things to consider before you choose your agent.

In this chapter, I will discuss agent representation in more detail. Decide if you want to be represented rather than just accommodated.

A real estate office has a broker to supervise agents. A broker can represent you if they choose to but most of the time, they will ask one of their agents to do that job. An agent is licensed by the state after they have attended a certain number of classes and applied for a license. Real estate training can be limited or vast depending on the individual agent's experience and level of education.

A broker has to have more education and experience before they can obtain a broker's license. Every office must have a broker in order to sponsor agents. Every broker is responsible for supervising agents as well.

There is a difference in agents. Some are Realtors® and some are not. Realtors® belong to the local association of Realtors®, the State Association of Realtors®, and the National Association of Realtors®.

Realtors® abide by a Code of Ethics. You can view the Code of Ethics online with a quick search.

For agents to follow the guidelines of the Code of Ethics, and be held accountable for actions, has proven to be quite valuable to the public. The trademark for Realtors® is used by Realtors® only. When you see this trademark sign, you will know those agents chose a higher standard in doing business.

Here you see the Realtor® logo and an MLS logo. MLS stands for Multiple Listing Service. It means anyone who displays this sign has access to all the home listings in your area.

You want to work with a Realtor® that works with all the other offices in your town. You will want someone who is knowledgeable about all the homes that are for sale, so you will have more choices and a better opportunity to get the best deal. Your Realtor® will show you homes listed for sale in their office and homes listed for sale in other offices at the same time. More choices equal more opportunities.

This sign means everyone has an equal opportunity for housing. No discrimination! This is a federal law. Agents must not discriminate against anyone because of race, color, religion, sex, national origin, handicap, or familial status. The Fair Housing Act was enacted in 1968.

There is also a law for Fair Credit that forbids lenders from discriminating on the basis of race, color, religion, national origin, sex, marital status or age. It also keeps lenders from discriminating based on income derived from public assistance.

So, if you want to buy a house and you have the down payment, closing costs, income sufficient to make the payments, and your credit score is good, you have a very good chance of becoming a new home owner. If it is your dream, to own instead of renting, let's get started making the dream come true.

*****

Most people know Realtors® or agents in their area. Some people call the name on the for sale sign in the yard of a property they like. What is the best way to choose an agent to represent you? Why is it important to have someone to Represent you? What does **Representation** mean? Is it that important? Let's discuss.

Representation means someone is speaking or acting on behalf of another person. In real estate transactions, there are 2 basic types of representation. Your agent is a buyer representative or a seller representative. You need a buyer agent, someone to represent you and your interests. You need someone to help you get the best deal.

When you sign a buyer agency agreement, you are entering into a legally binding contract with your agent. You are promising to be loyal to that agent and to work only with this one agent per this one transaction.

The agent is promising to provide agency services to you and the contract creates a *fiduciary relationship*. The fiduciary relationship is defined as a relationship where one party places special trust, confidence and reliance in a party to the contract. The other party has a legal duty to act for the benefit of the client. When you sign a buyer agency agreement, you are no longer just a customer but you are now a *client*. Those two words have very different meanings.

Confidentiality is a key component of a fiduciary relationship. When you tell your agent personal things, you want it to remain confidential. For example, suppose you only have 2 weeks to make a decision to buy a home. Time is precious to you.

This urgency should not be shared with the listing agent on any home you are considering buying. Otherwise, the other agent will know you are desperate and they will not be inclined to negotiate as easily on behalf of the seller. Knowing this personal information could cost you money.

It is important to have a buyer agent that represents you only and confidentiality is part of the service being offered. Other things you get with buyer agency are loyalty, obedience, disclosure, accountability and reasonable care.

Obedience means the agent will do what you ask. For example, you tell your agent to offer a specific amount and the agent is bound by law to offer the amount you requested. They cannot change anything without your permission. They represent you and your interests above anyone else, even themselves.

Disclosure means they disclose to you anything they know about a property or the seller of the property, which could give you an advantage in negotiations. Accountability is the ability to hold them responsible for their actions. Fiduciary relationship is very important and you only get it if you enter into this agreement with your agent.

Everything in real estate needs to be in writing! As a first-time home buyer, please remember this. If it is in writing, you can go back and read again and again. Do not make the mistake of hurrying and not putting everything in writing.

Do emails and texts have the same significance as a paper document? In 1999, The Uniform Electronic Transaction Act became law in every state but Illinois, Washington, New York, and Puerto Rico. In 2017, they also joined the Act. Each state is different, but in many states electronic signatures can be used for real estate transactions.

The Act does not differentiate between emails or texts. However, best practices use email more because texts can be lost much easier than emails. The law requires that a writing will be satisfied by an electronic record or electronic signature.

Most people communicate by email or texts today. This is why I am sharing the electronic act with you. Be aware of what you write or agree to in an email or text. It can be legally binding.

Chapter 5

Finding The Right Agent

Many people know licensed agents in their area. It may be a friend or relative that works in real estate. Don't choose your agent just because they are friends or relatives. Agents have different levels of education and experience. Their knowledge can save you money or cost you money with your transaction.

You are hiring someone to represent your interests in a purchase transaction. You want someone who cares enough to do a good job. You want someone who has knowledge and experience and will work hard for you.

Communication is so important and a good agent is quick to return phone calls and to communicate in various ways. In real estate transactions, timing is everything. That is why you need someone who takes communication very serious.

Residential real estate agents often work nights and weekends. It is not a 9 to 5 job. (Some lenders also work nights and weekends.)   You may be looking to buy a home in a seller's market, meaning there are less homes on the market at this time and the competition to buy them is fierce. There may be multiple offers on a home and timing is very important. You can miss a good deal in minutes. I have seen this happen numerous times.

You may be looking at homes for a month, and find the perfect place. You are dreaming of everything you and your family will enjoy with this home. You rush back to the office to write a contract. You get all the paperwork signed and your agent sends it over to the other agent that has the home listed for sale. The other agent sadly tells your agent the home just went under contract and the contract looks solid. You missed out by minutes.

This is why good communication is vital. An experienced agent will know which homes are being shown, how often, and how hot the market is in an area.

You may also be looking in a time of a buyer's market. A buyer's market is good for you because there are more homes available than buyers to buy them. You can get your best deal during a buyer's market. If there are a lot of foreclosures on the market, the price of individual seller owned homes are also lower. However, you may not want to wait until that happens. It can take years for the market to turn either way.

In 2020, the economy was roaring until the Covid-19 virus came and shutdown the country. To the surprise of many, during a pandemic, real estate sales have been on record scale. Many people decided to move out of big cities and into the suburbs or rural areas that are not so heavily populated. This is not a normal market situation.

When everything opens again, the economy could roar back, or it could nose dive. It may take a while to see which direction it takes. We will have to wait and see what happens. Many people used forbearance during the beginning of the pandemic to delay payment of their monthly mortgages. When the forbearance runs out and the people have to repay the amounts owed, many will let their homes be foreclosed and this will change local markets. More foreclosures mean lower house prices.

On the other hand, there has been very little home construction happening for the past decade especially in low and moderate income level homes. Some of the big tract builders went bankrupt in the 2008 recession and they have not comeback into business. This created a short supply of homes in these price ranges.

Most new home buyers will be looking in the low to moderate income price ranges. So, even in a time when the economy is not that great, the lack of supply is still dictating the price of homes. So you can see, you may end up in a multiple offer situation and this is where having the best agent means the difference in winning the bid, getting the home you want, and getting the best price.

As mentioned earlier, agents that belong to the local, state and national associations of Realtors® and pledge to abide by the Code of Ethics are held to a higher standard. I have been a Realtor® for many years. The Code of Ethics is over 100 years old and is updated periodically. Agents must take continuing education of the Code of Ethics when they renew their licenses.

A good agent will have the **education** they need to do a good job for you. They will have **experience** dealing with the public and dealing with other agents. They will be knowledgeable of the area in which you are looking to buy. They will know the market historically and Today! They will be available to you. They will communicate regularly. They will represent you and your best interests.

They will be **pleasant to work with,** but most of all, they will be **trustworthy**. You must be able to trust this person with personal private details about your life. If the person you are working with does not fit this description, get someone else.

As discussed in the previous chapter, you need to work with only one agent. Representation is about *loyalty, disclosure, obedience, confidentiality, accountability and reasonable care. These things make up what we call a **Fiduciary Relationship**.*

When you are in a Fiduciary Relationship you have confidentiality. What you say to your agent is confidential and will not be passed on to the seller or seller's agent. For an example, when looking at homes suppose you say to your agent, "This home is everything we want and need, I could give full price but let's offer 10% less for now."

That is a reasonable statement. You would expect your agent not to tell the seller or seller's agent what you said. It could cost you money. A fiduciary relationship keeps this from happening.

How do you get a fiduciary relationship? You sign a buyer's agent contract. Your agent then will represent you and you alone in your transaction.

Choose an agent by interviewing them like you would interview anyone for a job position. Find out what kind of experience they have, let them give you a presentation or resume' of their skills, get references and call the references. Were these clients happy with their buyer agent and why? Don't hesitate to ask questions.

This agent will be working for you, on your behalf. You want the best you can get. Find out what specialties they bring to the table. What education do they have, and what designations do they hold? You want someone who has good **negotiating skills** to get you the best deal. The references you talk to will help you decide who to choose as your buyer agent. Negotiating is a learned skill and not every agent is as skilled as another. Past clients sometimes will tell you how hard their agent negotiated on their behalf.

Reputation says a lot in the real estate industry. Ask and you will find out about an agent's reputation. It is important to hear what other clients have to say about the agent you are considering using to represent your interests.

Of the things mentioned, communication, education, experience, buyer agreement, negotiating skills, and reputation, which is most important? All of them are important. You want to work with the best agent and when you find that agent, you can begin your search for the perfect house.

*****

You have completed the first three steps.

1. You have defined the dream, what you want and need in a home.

2. Getting your credit in order and knowing your scores. Choosing a lender and getting a pre-approval letter.

3. Finding the best agent to work with and getting buyer representation.

Now you are better prepared. You are ready for

step number 4,

finding your dream home.

Chapter 6

Reality Begins with Home Search

Reality is making the dream come true. You have done the hard part. You have now completed 3 of the 4 steps in the process of buying your new home. **Step 4** is finding the home you have been dreaming of. It is the most fun part of the whole process.

It will be fun but also lots of work. Now you have a team to help you. Your Realtor®, your loan officer, your inspectors and title company are all a part of your team. If you have followed these steps, you are now ready to begin to look for your home.

Many, many people do not follow this plan. They decide on the spur of the moment to buy a house.

They see a for sale sign in the yard of a home they like and call the number on the sign. That number belongs to the selling agent. They are representing the seller in the sale of that home. Do you want to work with someone who is not representing you? They are on the other side, the side you are going to negotiate with. Don't be like these people. Follow the guide and do it right. You will then have a team on your side to help you with finding the right home, making sure it is in good condition and getting the best price. You will also have the title company protecting your interests.

You and your spouse or partner will enjoy seeing homes and learning about each one. You may have a few tense moments when one of you like a home and the other one does not. All in all though, it is the fun part. Discovering new places, new things, dreaming and imagining yourselves in each home you visit.

You will get to know your Realtor® and they will get to know you. You will learn of new neighborhoods, study areas for shopping, schools, transportation, government services, utility companies, parks, roadways, restrictions, home owner associations, and much more. It is a time of discovery and exploration. I call it adventure.

In today's covid-19 era, there will be more and more video visits to homes before you go visit the homes in person. People are scared, and many precautions are being taken to prevent the spread of the virus. You will need to wear a mask and maybe gloves or shoe coverings when entering a home. You will be advised not to touch things. Doors will be open and cabinet doors should also be open to allow you to see inside without touching. Your Realtor® will advise you on what to do.

Please do not bring children or parents or friends on initial visits. Most home owners want to keep the visitors to a minimum until they know for sure you have a real interest in buying their home. After you make your choice, you will have time to bring the family to view and give their approval.

Family approvals are important but they often result in hurt feelings. Be aware not everyone sees things like you do. Parents often point out things you did not see or consider. It may or may not be important to you. Children need to be happy in the home you have chosen also, but they usually are if they have their own space.

Buyer's remorse is something that is very real. Most people have buyer's remorse the day after they sign a purchase offer and get it accepted. This is normal. You will second guess yourself almost every time you buy a new house. Realtors® have the same problem. It is human nature. It will pass, usually in a day or two.

If it does not pass, you still have a way to get out of the contract if you bought some time with an **option period**. I have always urged my clients to buy an option period. Make it long enough to get all the inspections you think you will want to have completed. This gives you time to think about your decision and also time to get other inspections you did not think you needed at the beginning. Your agent will probably suggest 10-15 days.

Finding a home you and your family agree on may happen quickly or it may take time. The list you made in the beginning will determine which homes are considered in the running. You may have several choices and each home offfers different amenities.

Likely, no home will have everything on your list. No home is perfect either. Don't try to find perfection or you will be disappointed. Find the home that most closely matches your needs and wants. If it satisfies everyone in the family, that's the one to choose.

So, you now write the **purchase offer** and your Realtor's® job is to get the offer accepted by the seller. This is where their negotiating skills pay off. Most times, the offer will come back and forth a couple of times until everything in the offer is agreed upon. When final agreement happens and there are signatures and initials in every space, your offer has now become a **contract**. A legally binding contract, and the clock begins to tick.

Every contract has **time limits and deadlines** that must be met to the minute, such as 5:00 pm certain day of the month and year. Most contracts today, have an option period like I have already discussed. It will allow the buyer to back out for any reason. During this time period, the buyer can have inspections made on the property to find anything that is wrong with the home, the garage, and outbuildings. This is the time to get a copy of the subdivision restrictions and HOA rules, if applicable.

The average option period is about 10 days but can be longer. It is a negotiable item. You need time for inspections, but remember the seller does not want to wait a long time for you to say, "Yes, I am buying the house."

Home inspections will be done by a licensed and bonded inspector and they will give you a complete report with pictures. It will cost you about $400-500. You may want other inspections, like a water well inspection and report, or a septic inspection, if property is in the country. In some areas, hydrostatic inspections are required for plumbing. Pest inspections are most important to know the house is not being eaten by termites or wood ants. A roof inspection or a foundation inspection separate from the home inspection may also be warranted. Each property is different and requires different things.

Your home inspector is someone you choose, so you will need to check out the inspectors reputation before you choose one. Your Realtor® will give you a list of inspectors in your area. Most of them are good at explaining how things work in your new prospective home. They will show you personally how to operate all systems in the house. They will point out anything that is not working properly. They will explain all the defects the home has. Every home will have some deficiencies. No home is perfect, and the inspector will work hard to find all problems. The defects are judged by the inspector as something that must be repaired if it is a health and safety issue. Or it could be something that will need attention at a later date. You should listen carefully to your inspector, so you can gain as much knowledge about your new home as possible.

A seller's disclosure form should have been given to you before you signed the contract but if not, get it and study it. The seller is required to disclose any problems they are aware of, or repairs that have been made in recent years. The seller's disclosure is legally binding in court and should be kept. Your home inspection report should match with the seller's disclosure acknowledgment.

Once your inspections are done and you are satisfied with the home you have chosen to buy, you will begin working harder with your lender to get your loan approved. The lender will need a copy of the contract. You should give them the contract once it is signed, don't wait until after the option period is over. If you decide to back out of the contract during the option period, the lender can change to another contract.

You will be working with the lender during the whole process. They may ask for more documentation. Get it to them as soon as you can. Delays can cost you. There are deadlines in the contract to have your loan approved for closing. If you go beyond this time period, the seller must agree in writing to extend the contract. If you are in a seller's market, there are other people waiting for your contract to fail, so they can buy the house you want to buy. Provide the documents your lender needs immediately. Sometimes, you will provide the same document more than once. Don't ask why, just do it.

The title company will time stamp your contract when it comes in. They will immediately begin to look at the title for any deficiencies. They may contact you several times during the process. The whole process could take between one to three months from beginning to closing.

Closings are often held at the title company. The seller will sign final documents and the buyer will sign final documents at different times usually, but on the same day. All documents are dated on the same day and this is very important. Often, one of the parties to a contract is in a different location. Title companies work with other title companies to make the transaction happen. Sometimes, only one title company is involved and they will use a mobile notary to meet with the out of area party. Then, documents are emailed and snail mailed to the closing agent.

You will get keys at closing if the seller has already moved out. You can celebrate now. You are officially a **Home Owner** when the deed is delivered to you.

*****

Let's go back over the steps.

Step 1 Defining the Dream

What is the dream? What do you really want? Make your lists of needs and wants. Compromise. Discuss. Think it through thoroughly. Don't hesitate to dream. Many people think owning a home is out of the question and they suppress their dreams. Nothing ever comes about unless you dream first. So let your dreams out. Speak them out. Share your dreams.

Step 2 How to pay for the home

Get your credit scores and improve them, if necessary. Find a mortgage lender and get pre-approved for a loan. Use a lender that you can meet in person, someone that you can trust. Find a person that is easy to talk to, that will take the time to get to know you. Choose a lender that is available to take your calls or emails. My favorite lender will answer my calls even at night and on weekends.

Step 3 Find the right agent

By interviewing, and researching agents and offices, you will find the best agent for you. Sign a buyer's representation agreement. You need someone to represent you and look out for your best interests. A buyer's agreement gives you a fiduciary relationship.

Step 4 Home search

The search begins for the perfect place for you and your family. This is the fun part. It is a time of learning about different homes and neighborhoods. It is also a time for big decisions, choosing which home is best. Once a home is chosen, the agent and loan officer will guide you through the process. The inspector can relieve your fears or not with the inspection report.

*****

These four steps will bring you to the perfect house. If you have come this far, you now have a buyer's agent to guide you through the rest of the transaction. There will be lots of papers to sign and decisions to make during the whole transaction and your agent will be in contact with you often.

Your mortgage lender will lead you through the process of being approved for your loan. They will be calling from time to time to keep you updated on the progress of your loan. They will also call for more documents from time to time.

The title company is working to make sure the title to your new property has no clouds on the title. They may call occassionally with a question or two. They will arrange for the closing and set appointment times for the seller and the buyer to come in to sign final documents.

This is Your Team, the Realtor®, the loan originator, and the title company. They are all working on your behalf. They will be with you throughout the process.

The inspector is also on your team but is only there during the time the inspections are being made. You may still call the inspector if questions arise later.

Your Team consists of many players including people behind the scenes but there are a few very important members. **Your agent** is the most important. As we discussed in Chapter 5, choosing the right agent means the difference in the kind of deal you get. Choosing the right agent will make the process smooth and less painful.

Choosing the right agent will give you peace of mind. Choosing the right agent will help the process feel like fun. Your agent will coordinate all activities.

You will have your questions professionally answered and have the confidence everything is happening on time with deadlines. Your agent will be watching out for your interests. So, taking the time to research agents and getting buyer representation will be worth the extra time upfront.

Your loan originator is another important member of your team. Your loan originator will walk you through a complicated process and you will be relying on this person for updates. Every time another document is needed, your loan originator will be reaching out to you. You will be talking to them often.

Following their instructions carefully will result in faster service. Your loan originator is watching out for you also. They are doing their best to help you get the loan. They have helped you decide which kind of loan to apply for and answered all your questions concerning the differences. They constantly keep you updated. They will be working with the loan processors and underwriter.

The title company will occassionally reach out to you as well. When the **title commitment** is received from the title company, be sure to read it. It is a commitment from the title company saying they will issue a title policy on the property with possible exceptions. If you do not understand anything in it, please contact your agent for clarification. Your agent should have already read it, anticipating any questions from you.

Make sure all the names are correct and spelled right. Make sure there is nothing on Schedule B or C you do not understand. Sometimes, there are problems listed here. If your agent cannot answer your questions, call the title company. They will be glad to help. There is a place in the contract that allows you a certain number of days to dispute anything in the title commitment. **This is a deadline.** Make sure you look at this commitment immediately and stay within the deadlines.

The title company will prepare the closing statement. Your agent should have given you an estimated buyer's closing sheet when you signed the contract. This was only an estimate but it should be fairly close to the final closing statement.

You will not get the final statement until a couple days before closing. If there is anything on it you do not agree with, call your agent.

This chapter contains a recap of all you need to make your dream a reality in a short version. The following chapters will take each step into more detail.

Section Two

Chapter 7

Loans and Your Originator

Your loan originator is your key to obtaining your loan. It can be an easy process or a very difficult one. Having a loan originator that you trust, can take away a lot of stress when you know they are working hard for you. It is important to work with someone that is knowledgeable and experienced. I prefer someone that is local, so we can meet face to face. There are so many questions over a period of time, face to face meetings are better for me. You may prefer everything online but a face to face relationship is often more efficient.

Tony Stevenson is a loan originator in the San Antonio and Texas Hill Country area. He is the kind of loan officer I can depend on. I have sent many clients to Tony over the years and my clients have given him rave reviews. He is always accessible and eager to help clients. He is great at explaining things to first-time homebuyers.

I asked Tony to share with first-time home buyers things he thought they needed to know. **Here is Tony's response.**

Is the process to buy a home difficult? I am sure that's what most first-time home buyers (FTB's) think, especially when it comes to qualifying for a mortgage. About 67% of Americans think you have to give 20% down to qualify for a mortgage according to NerdWallet 2019 Home Buyer Report. Most FTB's think the same thing but most only make a 6%-7% down payment.

How much down payment will you need? What loan programs are available for you? First-time home buyers may qualify for assistance from many different state programs, some tax breaks, and federally backed loans such as FHA. FHA is the most popular as it is designed with a 3.5% down payment. However, there are loan programs that offer a zero down payment. One example, is the USDA program for rural communities. There are also other down payment assistance programs that vary from city to city and state to state.

The process to buy a home is not difficult. The first piece of advice I would give is to find a "Local" real estate agent and lender. Not faceless internet providers but real live people who know the area where you want to begin your home search. If you have not chosen a lender, your real estate agent may be able to guide you. They will refer you to a lender who they trust that will walk you through the process from application to closing.

If the agent refers you to an internet lender, run, don't walk to another agent. All that agent is doing is referring you to a lender they have no actual relationship with and whom they may be receiving money for referrals.

Before you begin your search for a home you need to do the following:

1. Find a lender. Someone you can trust, with an excellent reputation in the community in which you are going to begin your home search.

2. Get pre-qualified. Better yet, get pre-approved for a mortgage. This lets you know what price home you can afford and which loan program to use. There is no sense in looking at homes you cannot afford.

The difference between a pre-qualification and pre-approval is this: Getting pre-qualified means the lender has determined your qualifications only on the basic information you provided them on the application with no substantial proof or documentation. A pre-approval means the lender has reviewed your income, assets, and credit information using documentation such as paystubs, tax returns, copies of cash asset accounts, etc.

3. Once pre-qualified or pre-approved, get a letter from the lender to give to your real estate agent. Now, you may start looking for a home. Without the letter, most real estate agents will not want to show you homes. They want to know you are ready to buy.

4. After you find a home you like, my advice is to spend an hour or two there in the evening or at different times during the day. Listen for air traffic, road traffic, and neighborhood noise. Talk to neighbors and ask them how they like the neighborhood. Is there anything they think you should know? There's nothing worse than to move into a home and find out there is a flight pattern at 3:00 AM that wakes you up regularly. Surprises like this are not fun. Research the neighborhood, it is important to find out everything that concerns you.

5. After getting the executed sales contract, be sure your agent **gets a copy of the contract to your lender as soon as possible**.

6. Finish getting all remaining documents to your lender. This is crucial to obtaining an on-time closing. Nobody likes a closing to be delayed for any reason. But, don't get frustrated because things don't always go as planned.

   Your lender should keep you and your real estate agent informed as to progress during the lending process. There are issues that could come up such as: Did the home pass inspection? Your real estate agent will know this. Is there a survey that can be used or do you need a new survey? Are there any other inspections required such as water well, septic, termite, etc? Did the home appraise for value? Your agent and lender should be able to answer any questions or concerns.

7. Do not make any major purchases or quit your job during the loan process. Keep current on all your debts/bills. Don't make any large money bank transfers without letting your lender know first. You will need

proof where your funds are coming from to close. All lenders require this kind of proof. "Mattress money" doesn't count.

8. By this time (after appraisal) you should have loan approval from the lender. If there are any remaining underwriting conditions needed, be sure to provide whatever the lender needs as soon as possible. Time is crucial.

9. If all goes well, you can close on your home and schedule to move in. Schedule your closing with your real estate agent. DO NOT schedule movers unless your lender has your loan approved and you are scheduled to close.

10. Congratulations! You are now a homeowner.

Words to live by during the entire process before and after:

Be sure you have a nest egg (money saved) for unforeseen expenses such as appliances, curtains, lawn care, emergencies, etc.

Finally, you never know what life is going to throw at you. Always try to be prepared. Mistakes can and will happen. Be patient. Work through problems with your real estate agent and lender. Remember, your real estate agent is the one person who can help direct you during the home buying process. Do not forget to go Local! It is exciting to buy a home, Good luck and have fun.

Tony Stevenson, Loan Officer

Tony Stevenson has given some valuable insight here. Tony has worked in the mortgage origination field for over thirty years and helped many first-time home buyers through the process. He is experienced and a well-known leader in his area.

Hopefully, you will find someone like Tony to work with when searching for a mortgage lender. The process goes much easier when you have a lender you can talk with easily and you fully trust that person. Knowing you have a friend that is working hard for you at all times and that you are not just a number means a lot.

I have bought and sold a very large number of homes over my forty year career. There were times I had a mortgage lender that did not work for me unless I had them on the phone. They were jumping through hoops then, but when I hung up, I knew it was just a show. If I did not constantly call them and persuade them, I received no service.

Many times, I had to do their job or the transaction would not have happened. As a Realtor®, this is so aggravating. People do not realize how valuable a Realtor® is at times. I can name multiple transactions that would have ended in the trash can, had I not stepped in and did the work the lender was supposed to do.

Take Tony's advice, hire a mortgage lender that you can talk to face to face, or directly on the phone or by email. It is easier to deal with one person than a whole group of people. Develop a personal, professional relationship with the lender if you want the best service. Choose someone "Local" that values and supports the community in which you want to live.

Chapter 8

The Contract Form

Every state is different, but I worked in Texas and we use promulgated contract forms whenever possible. These forms come from the Texas Real Estate Commission or from the Texas Association of Realtors®. I am sure many states do similar things as Texas. You will need to check with Realtors® in your area to see what is acceptable. All Texas Realtors® use promulgated forms.

Promulgated forms are prepared by a group of attorneys that work for the Texas Real Estate Commission or Texas Association of Realtors®. I have rarely found an instance where there was not a form for any situation in our files. The commission tries to cover every scenario with a form for its members to use. Doing this, they are lessening the opportunity for mistakes by agents.

In Texas, you may hire an attorney to prepare a contract for you if you wish. Most people do not go this way unless the transaction is unusual in some way, or contains a large parcel of land. Land contracts often use an attorney prepared form instead of a promulgated form.

As a licensed agent, we are allowed to fill in the blanks. We are not allowed to practice law by designing our own forms or changing the ones provided to us. You can rest assured the forms being used are legal and the attorneys try to cover every angle in each transaction.

The outside edges of each page are boundaries in a contract form. Whatever is written inside those boundaries are part of the form and nothing else.

Every blank space should have something written in it, even if it is a dash or a zero. I make sure I leave nothing blank. When signed by all parties and dated, the contract form is **legally binding!**

Do not sign anything you do not understand. Get an attorney to explain it to you if needed. Your signature is your agreement to everything that is written in the contract form. Every page is initialed at the bottom indicating you have read and agreed to what is written on the page. The signature page at the end is formal proof of your agreement to the terms that have been expressed in writing.

The whole agreement must be in writing. This is so important! Do not take anyone's word that something will be done. Get it in writing and have it signed by all parties.

*****

Let's assume you have never seen a contract form to purchase a home. Again, I will use Texas as an example. If you wanted to purchase a home in Texas right now, your Realtor® would use the TREC NO. 20-14 form also known as the One To Four Family Residential Contract (Resale) form. It consists of 10 pages.

Each page has numbered paragraphs and some paragraphs contain alphabetical letters addressing different things concerning the particular subject of the paragraph.

For instance in Paragraph 1. Parties, the names of the sellers and buyers are listed. It is important that all names are spelled correctly. The title company uses the legal names listed here to prepare documents.

*****

In Paragraph 2. Property, a legal description is given, and the address of the subject property. Paragraph 2 has 5 different lettered sections. All these are important and should be read. Everything written in the contract is of importance. Read your contract carefully. Ask questions if you do not understand something. Section D of Paragraph 2. lists anything the seller is retaining that would normally pass to the buyer. Examples are window coverings, a mirror that was fixed in place, or a chandelier that has sentimental value. Pay attention to this area.

In section E of Paragraph 2 Reservations, it discusses reservations like oil, gas, minerals and more. It says an attached addendum is needed for this. If there are reservations, make sure it is written on the proper addendum.

*****

Addendums are extra forms that are made a part of the contract form itself. So, instead of having 10 pages, you may have several addendums. Your complete contract may include 20 pages or more if you have addendums. The complete contract is escrowed at the title company when all parties have signed.

Addendums are attached to the contract and made at the same time, not later. An addendum made later might be approved or not. The seller does not have to agree to anything after the initial contract is signed. So, make your offer once and include everything the first time. Changes to a contract must be approved by all parties and of course, there is an addendum for that.

All states are different, but in Texas there is a **Non-Realty Items Addendum** I need to mention. If you want to keep the refrigerator, washer, dryer, or anything not built-in, you must write this addendum and make it a part of the contract. Otherwise, these items may be retained by the seller, even if they were listed in the MLS sheet as part of the house.

*****

Paragraph 3. Sales Price is one of the most important ones.

A. Cash portion of sales price (down payment)
$_____

B. SUM of all financing (Loans)
$_____

C. Sales Price (add A to B = C)
$_____

We will not go through the whole contract as your agent will explain this to you. Every state has different forms. There are some things that remain the same for making a legal contract.

The names, description of the property, the sales price and financing needed, earnest money on Paragraph 5, title policy, and survey. Paragraph 7 is property condition, then repairs, closing date on Paragraph 9, possession, settlement expenses, prorations, notices, added addendums, termination option, attorney if requested. The signatures of parties is on page 8 below Paragraph 24.

As you can see, the contract form is thorough. As a first-time home buyer, you are trusting your agent to explain things to you. There is a lot to know and you may not completely understand all that is involved. This is the reason for choosing a good agent that truly represents you and your interests. Ask questions. Be informed.

*****

In Paragraph 5, the earnest money is discussed. **What is earnest money?** It is an amount of money put down with the contract as a show of good faith. This is saying, "I will go through with the contract if the seller accepts my offer. Here is part of my down payment in a show of good faith." You are "putting your money where your mouth is," as many would say.

The earnest money is held by the title company until closing. Then it becomes part of the down payment.

For example, if the down payment was $10,000 and the earnest money was $2,000, at closing you would owe the remainder of $8,000 plus closing costs.

Why is this necessary? In theory, the buyer may lose the earnest money if they back out of the contract and do not close. This compensates the seller when they have removed their home from the market during the time the buyer is working to close the transaction. It may take a month or two to finish the loan approval or other requirements. The seller is waiting and hoping the transaction will close. If the deal does not close, the seller will receive the earnest money as damages.

There are lots of reasons why the buyer may retain the earnest money in cases where the deal doesn't close. One is loan approval. Sometimes, but not always the buyer keeps the earnest money if loan approval is not obtained. Your agent will explain all of this to you.

The addendum discussing loan approval has deadlines to protect the buyer and the seller. The offer you make will be the offer you agree to abide by. This addendum has blanks that will be filled in with a number of days the buyer has to get approvals. Make the time periods in addendums long enough and anticipate delays. This is where your loan origination officer can help. They know how long it will take. Use their advice.

Sellers want transactions to close as soon as possible. Often, there are multiple offers on the table. The seller will choose the best offer. Your agent will help you decide on the number of days in each area of the contract to make it more appealing to the seller. However, give yourself enough time to get everything done. Contracts fall apart many times, because the deadlines came too quickly and sellers were not willing to re-negotiate. It is a delicate balance. Your agent and loan officer need to be on the same page.

I am not going through the entire contract form in this book as each state's forms are different. I do want to point out a few more things I deem very important for first-time home buyers to understand.

*****

In Paragraph 7, Property Condition B. discusses the **seller's disclosure notice**. A seller's disclosure notice is a form the seller acknowledges that contains any information about the property. It will list all the items the property contains such as appliances, heating and air conditioning systems, public water and sewer lines and a host of other things. It also tells the buyer of anything that needs repair or that has been repaired. The seller says this information is correct to the best of their belief and signs the document. It is a legally binding document.

You should get the seller's disclosure notice from your agent as you are viewing properties. This way you can better determine the value of a property before you make an offer. Whether you have received the seller's disclosure notice or not, you will mark one of 3 boxes in this area of the contract form.

Some of the things that could make a difference in the amount of money you offer for a home, is whether there has been a fire at the property in the past. Or whether, a structure or fence is on a property line, or even if a meth lab existed on the property at one time. Things of this nature are very important and can affect the new buyer in ways they never imagined. A seller's disclosure notice is a valuable document that can help you decide if you want to buy a property or how much you are willing to pay.

*****

In Paragraph 9, you will place the date of your **closing**. In Paragraph 10, you will decide on the date of your **possession** of the property. Do not assume you get the keys to your new home on the day you close unless you put that in your offer to purchase. Moving day is filled with anxiety for everyone. Make sure everyone is on the same page and someone is not moving out at the same time someone else is moving in unless you don't mind the chaos.

The seller is usually waiting for the funds from closing to close the transaction on their new home. Closings like this are called double closings and can happen on the same day. Everything has to be highly calculated and planned for simultaneous closings. Sometimes, the seller has removed their furnishings by closing day and sometimes, not. What you negotiate at the time of your offer is what will happen.

As a buyer, you will want to walk-thru your new home before you sign papers. This walk-thru occurs the day of or the day before closing. If the seller has moved out and during the move something was damaged, you will want it repaired or to be compensated for the damage. This problem could cause a delay in closing. You must remain flexible because this a stressful time. This rarely happens, but it does happen. That is why I am preparing you today for the worst but hoping for the best.

Chapter 9

Termination Option and Inspections

One of the most important parts of your contract form is the **Termination Option**. If you want to **buy a few days of time** to do your inspections and arrange financing or whatever, you may. You will give the seller an amount of option money, usually a small fee for this privilege. In Texas, an average option period is about 10 days. The fee can be as little as $100 or as much as you and the seller agree upon.

The average time period and fee is totally negotiable. I have seen option periods for up to 30 days long. I have also seen option amounts up to $10,000. So, this is an area of the contract where you can be creative depending on what you are buying and what the seller is expecting. Average homes, average transactions do not vary much but in special cases, be creative.

During the option time period you have the right to cancel the contract and back out for any reason, or no reason at all. The seller has agreed to take your offer at this point and you are in a contract, but you still have a right to back out. Your option money is **non-refundable,** unlike the earnest money. The seller retains it no matter what. You will do inspections during this time. If something is found to be wrong with the house and you no longer wish to purchase, you may back out and receive your earnest money.

Termination options are great. Knowing what you are buying by doing inspections is imperative. Have a termination option and do inspections. If you need to re-negotiate the contract after you get the inspections, the termination option gives you the leverage to do that.

When the option period runs out, if you have not terminated the contract, it goes forward. Your earnest money is now at risk if you back out. You could also be sued if you back out for no reason. Following the deadlines in a contract is very important. That is why the legal term **'Time is of the essence'** is written in every contract.

Termination options can be used for a variety of things. Inspections are the most common. However, they may also be used in cases where a family member has not seen a property and another family member wants to make an offer before that can happen. Maybe, someone is out of town and property is selling quickly. To avoid losing a property, one family member writes an offer contingent on the approval of the other family member.

Another case could be a question of money that is not available immediately such as in a trust fund. Having a termination option secures the right to purchase without losing a large amount of money, if situations do not go as intended.

Inspections are the biggest reason to buy a termination option. You will have this time period to do a home inspection. When you hire a licensed and bonded home inspector, all systems in the home are inspected. These will include electrical, plumbing, roof, and foundation. If anything looks wrong with any of these, the inspector will recommend further investigation of problems and repairs. There will always be a number of minor issues with any home inspection report. These are easily negotiated with the seller for repair or replacement. The bigger issues are the ones you should be most interested in fixing or maybe, backing out of the contract if they are too serious.

If your new home is in the country, a septic and water well inspection will need to be done as well. Your home inspector may or may not have the licenses needed for these kind of inspections. A water sample should be sent to the county or state for analyzing.

The inspector will give you a report with photos of each area that has a specified problem or deficiencey as we discussed in Chapter 6. The report is quite lengthy. Many of the things you see in the report as a deficiency may have been perfectly fine at the time the house was built. As time goes on, codes change. Now, with updated building codes, some things that were fine then, are now a deficiency. This does not mean it has to be brought up to date. The inspector is simply making you aware. When you buy an older home, you must expect things like this to be on the report.

Then, there are items that need to be repaired. The inspector will point these out. If the items are a health hazard, they must be repaired before closing! Usually, the seller is responsible for these type items. You must negotiate all repairs with an addendum to the contract in writing. There may be other items that need repair that are not health hazards. These repairs are negotiable as well.

When you have a termination option, you have the power to get repairs paid by the seller. Otherwise, if you are not happy, you may walk away from the contract and get your earnest money back. Sometimes, the inspections will reveal problems you never dreamed about. They may be too large to deal with and you have the right to terminate the contract. You will only lose the amount of money you paid for the option period and the cost of the inspections.

This happens more often than you would imagine. Today, a large percentage of contracts terminate before closing. It is usually because of non-approval of loans, but it does happen sometimes because inspections revealed serious problems with the home.

Do the inspections. Talk to your inspector. Have the inspector show you the problems and discuss all the systems in the home. How do they work? How much life expectancy does each have currently? What would the cost of repairs be for any item needing repair? The inspector is happy to share these things with you. They work for you. You are paying for the service, so ask questions.

If you are successful in negotiating repairs, you must follow up and make sure the repairs are done in a reasonable amount of time. The appraisal should be done after the repairs if possible. Never close your transaction before repairs are completed. This might cause a problem that could only be fixed in court. It is better to make sure the repairs are done first. This is one reason you have a walk-thru before closing. You are agreeing the home is in the condition it was contracted to be in at closing. Once you sign the walk-thru, your rights are limited. You signed off on the deal.

Chapter 10

The Appraisal

The appraisal is the part of your transaction that will give you the most anxiety. By now, you have completed lots of the steps to home ownership. One of the few things remaining until your dreams are realized is the appraisal.

People get nervous when they have no control of a situation. This is what the appraisal is like, nerve-racking. You have absolutely no control of the appraisal. Appraisers are selected at random by the loan companies. An appraiser is usually from the area where the home is located but sometimes, the appraiser is not. If they are from a different area, they may not be as familiar as an appraiser from the local area. The choice is a random draw. You cannot be a part of the appraial.

The appraiser makes an appointment to view the home. They will draw an outline of the home, with measurements of each room. They will describe the home and the amenities in their report. They will compare the home with other homes that recently sold in the area. The appraiser contrasts the good and bad things about each property.

The report is thorough and takes several days to prepare. The appraisal is paid for by the buyer at closing. You will receive a copy of the report. It contains photos of each property. The home you are buying must appraise for at least the purchase price. If it does not, you must re-negotiate your contract. Usually, the seller will drop the price to the appraised value if they really want to sell.

On the other hand, if the appraised value comes back more than the purchase price, you have made a good deal and the seller must sell at the contracted price.

Appraisals are truly educated guesses. However, appraisers are well-educated and their reports carry a lot of weight. You can rarely contest an appraisal and be successful.

Loan companies lend based on the appraisal report. The appraiser is the loan companies' eyes and ears. The home is the collateral and must be valued at least for the purchase price.

Appraisers are in short supply these days. If a loan approval is delayed, it is often because the appraisal has not been completed. You may have to wait for several weeks for an appraiser because they are so busy.

You may check with your loan officer to see if the appraisal has been ordered. Or, if the appraisal has been done, but they are still waiting for the report. There are going to be times when you just need to know. It is a hard waiting time. Of course, you want to know as soon as possible if the appraised value has come in over or under the contract price.

The appraiser has access to the multiple listing services of the area. This is where a lot of information comes from about the compared properties that are found in the report. The appraiser may also drive by each property included and take their own photos. Most times, they find all they need online. Title companies may also provide some of the information listed in the report. Each report can contain 5-10 comparable homes.

There will be information about the community and other amenities in the neighborhood. A map showing each property's location is also inserted. The report contains square footage of each home, number of rooms, age, garages, out buildings, appliances, pools, fences, and even taxes. Homes are compared by all means possible.

Some things are not possible to compare equally, however. My home is insulated extremely well. I mean EXTREMELY well. It cost a lot more to build than most homes of the same size because of the quality, and the way it was constructed. Instead of regular roll fiberglass insulation, I have styrofoam insulation in my walls. The cold weather is kept out of my house, and my utility bills are a lot less because of the superior insulation.

The appraiser did not know this information when she appraised my home at the time I bought it. Would it have made a difference? No, if a home is insulated, it is insulated as far as value is concerned. Does it make a difference for me? YES! A big YES! It makes a difference in the comfort I have in my home and a difference in my utility bills. This is an amenity that goes with my home that few would recognize even exists.

Let's take countertops for another example. Does a granite countertop bring more value than a laminate, solid surface, or formica countertop? Yes, but are there different levels of quality in the granite? Yes, but a granite countertop is a granite countertop. Understand? It is not always apples to apples, but apples to oranges that get appraised.

There are so many things that could be discussed about appraisals but as a first-time home buyer, the biggest thing is to get it done quickly and hope the value is there. Once the appraisal is done, your loan can move to underwriting. Your loan officer knows the phases your loan goes through and where it is at most times. Give a call, if you want to know your loan phase.

Once the loan goes to the underwriter, the loan officer is anxiously waiting for approval. The loan can be approved as is, or the underwriter may want more information. Often, they need clarification on some aspect of the loan. You may be asked for another copy of a document you have already provided. The processed loan package may have some missing parts. The underwriter will go through the loan package and let you know if they need more documents.

They will prepare all the figures and this takes a few days. My loan officer has recently asked agents to use 60 days for approval. Things are moving slower than normal. A 30 day closing is not the average now during this 2020 pandemic.

As stated earlier, when an appraisal comes back lower than the contracted purchase price, the contract can be re-negotiated with the seller. Usually, the seller will lower the purchase price to match the appraised value. However, there are times the seller will not take less money. If this happens, the buyer has the option of paying the difference in cash if the buyer has the means to do so. The loan company will only make a loan for the loan to value ratio agreed based on the appraised value.

For example, you are getting a 95% loan and paying 5% down payment. The appraisal comes back $10,000 less than the purchase price. You would be asked to pay an additional $10,000, plus your 5% down payment. Most people cannot or will not do this, so the seller will usually lower the purchase price to match the apprasied value. If parties cannot agree, the contract ends and becomes null and void, if you checked the right place on the contract offer. Read every item on the contract. You need a clear understanding of what you are agreeing to concerning each aspect of the contract. Your agent should be helping you understand things like this. Do not hesitate to ask questions. Understand fully before signing.

Chapter 11

Taxes and Insurance

Property taxes are paid to your city, your county, your school district and many other entities. You may look up all kinds of information about taxes on your county's website. You will see the tax rate for each entity for any given year. The tax rate is multiplied by the assessed value of your home.

Assessed Value multiplied by (X) Tax Rate = Amount due at end of tax year.

The assessed value is not market value. It is a number the tax-assessor-collector uses when figuring taxes on a particular piece of property. You may call your local tax appraisal district and ask how they determine assessed value. It is less than market value. Market value is what your home would sell for, if it was on the market today.

There are deductions for various things. If your home is your primary residence, you may homestead it by signing a form and filing it with your county tax appraisal district. This will lower your taxes. You may also qualify to receive deductions if you are disabled, a military veteran, blind, or of a certain age. You need to go see your county tax assessor-collector to find out which ones you may qualify for.

Every year you will be sent a tax bill which is due at the end of the year. If your county has two bills each year, they will bill you twice. If you have a mortgage, chances are good you also have an escrow account. The mortgage company will receive the tax bill and pay it for you from your escrow account. This is very convenient. Just make sure the taxes are being paid every year.

There are only a few reasons someone can take your home. One reason is if you don't pay your mortgage. The other reason is if you do not pay your taxes. So, make sure both are paid on time.

Tax rates are determined by how much money is needed to run city and county governments. Projects the city and county are doing at any given time are also expenditures that are paid with tax dollars. There may be money needed for new road construction or water systems. Taxpayers pay for these type of infrastructure expenses by paying their property taxes.

School districts receive a large portion of tax dollars. Usually, the largest amount goes to the school district. The size of the district and amenities the schools provide determine tax rates. Attending school board meetings is a good way to see how they are spending your property tax money.

When considering buying your first home, you may want to consider what kind of community you want to live in. The more expenditures the city and county make, the higher your taxes will be even for property of the same value in another location.

Once a year, about 4 to 5 months before taxes are due, you will receive a notice of assessed value. The tax office is allowed to refigure your assessed value every year. If you have made improvements to your property, there will be an increase in assessed value if the tax office is aware of the improvements. This could be a new fence, a bigger driveway, a room addition or a variety of other things.

If you feel the increase is too much, you may gather information to refute their claim. You will make an appointment to go before the board and argue the increase. Many times, citizens win if they bring any kind of documentation to prove the increase is too much.

You may get information on comparable properties from your Realtor®, or you may compare property values on the county website. If you have made improvements, you could take receipts. Bring copies of documentation for each board member. Anything that will help you prove your points, makes your chances of winning the argument stronger and keeping your taxes low.

Taxes rarely increase very much per year, but over time those small increments can bring a property out of reasonable value. So, it is always good to watch where your values are, and correct them with a board review if necessary. There are time limits for reviewing property assessments, so check with the county for the times a homeowner is allowed to do this.

Insurance

Your homeowner's insurance is also paid by your mortgage company if you have an escrow account. Your insurance company will bill the mortgage company on your behalf, and they will pay it. This is another convenience of having an escrow account. If you need to change anything with your insurance, just contact your insurance agent and they can handle it for you.

Homeowner's insurance will pay for loss of your home or partial loss if by fire, wind, hail, or other hazards. Each policy is different. A portion of your home's contents is also insured under a homeowner's policy. For additional coverage, you must write a rider to the policy. Ask your agent what is covered and what is not covered. It is imperative to know now what is covered and not be surprised later if you have a claim.

Some areas will need flood insurance. Homeowner's insurance will not pay for water damage caused by rain and flooding. If you are in a flood zone, you need flood insurance. Your realtor® should show you flood maps, so you will be aware of the degree of flood risk before you contract to buy a home. Even if there are no waterways near your home, there still can be a flood risk. FEMA (Federal Emergency Management Agency) updates flood maps on a regular basis and insurance rates are affected by these maps. Ask to see one where your home is located.

Some areas need windstorm insurance. If you live on the coast, the threat of damaging winds is greater and some homes are required to have windstorm insurance.

Bundling your home and auto can save you some money. Having an escrow account is so convenient you may forget you are even paying insurance. It is a good idea to check coverage and rates every few years to make sure you are not paying too much.

From time to time, insurance or taxes may increase. When this happens, the amount of escrow money being added every month to your account will need to be adjusted. So, do not be surprised if at the end of a year, you get notice of an increase to your monthly mortgage because taxes or insurance rates have increased. This happens very rarely but it does happen.

Your escrow account must always have enough money in it to pay for taxes and insurance when they become due. There must be a cushion as well. Once the account is replenished, if you are paying too much per month, the mortgage payment will be adjusted down. This will be automatically handled by the mortgage company. It is nothing you need worry about. I am including this simply for your information, so you will not be surprised if it happens.

Chapter 12

Home Warranties

Home Warranties are wonderful for bringing a little peace of mind to new home owners. The warranties are good for one year and then can be renewed on a yearly basis if you desire. Most sellers will pay for a one year home warranty at closing.

There are many companies to choose from. You may choose the warranty and the company from whom it comes and put that in your contract offer. Or, you may simply state in your offer you want a home warranty.

They generally cost from $500 to $750 depending on the coverage you choose. You may also upgrade your warranty. They cover the cost of repair or replacement of a variety of fixtures, appliances or even water leaks inside a wall.

I had a terrible leak once inside a wall when a pipe broke. My home warranty repaired the leak and the walls where they had to remove sheetrock. They replaced the sheetrock on two sides, opposite walls, different rooms. They repainted the walls to match the rest of the room. I was so impressed with my company. They did an excellent job. I never knew how important a home warranty was until that happened. They replaced so much and the cost was way more than the policy cost. It was a good investment.

I have always used home warranty companies. Over the years I personally have had a dishwasher replaced, a water heater replaced and several repairs on air conditioning units. I believe home warranties are worth the money and the peace of mind. If the seller will pay for the first year, ask for it in the purchase offer.

Not all warranties are the same. I have told you about the pros. Now, let me tell you about the cons. Most home warranty companies have a list of contractors they hire to make repairs. The contractors are not always the best in the area. In fact, quite the opposite. They also get paid per visit. It is important to watch and see what they are doing. If they are not doing things right, contact the company and ask for a different contractor.

Home warranty companies are only as good as the local contractors they use. Ask your Realtor® about the different companies. Ask if the agent is getting a commission from the company for their recommendation. There are many companies to choose from but most areas have 3-4 that are the best.

Each trip that a contractor makes to your home will have a nominal fee. They are required to repair, or replace the item if it cannot be repaired. Often, an older dishwasher, water heater, refrigerator, washing machine or range cannot be repaired. Parts may not be available. If the contractor cannot get parts, they will replace the appliance with a similar model. It may not be the same brand, however. If brand names are important to you, you may be able to pay the difference and get the brand name you want.

Home warranty companies try hard to please the customer in my experience. They are selling something that is not a necessity. Their reputation in an area is very important to their success.

They will not pay for items that have been abused, or items not regularly maintained. So, it is important to change your air conditioning/heating filters as discussed in a different chapter. Maintain your home in good condition and you will actually save money.

Home warranties are a better deal for pre-owned homes. If you are buying a brand new home, you will get the manufacturer's warranties for appliances. You may also have a warranty from the builder, so a home warranty may not be as necessary as if you were buying an older home.

Some companies also have a "build-your-own" policy that allows you to add or delete items that will be covered. This will give you flexibility to make sure the things you are most concerned with are insured. Peace of mind is what home warranties are all about.

Chapter 13

Title Company and Closing

The title company will do a title search on the property you are planning to buy. They will find any errors in the chain of title and will help to cure it. They bring a wealth of knowledge to the transaction. You, as a purchaser will never know all the things they do. They will write a policy of title insurance to protect your title from previous owners or anyone claiming a right to your property.

The title policy is a very valuable asset. Without a title policy insuring your title is good with no liens or clouds, you cannot get a loan approved. The title company will issue you a title commitment a few days after they get a copy of your contract. When you close your transaction you will get the actual title policy.

The title policy is usually paid for by the seller but it is a negotiable item in the contract. The price of the policy is based on the price of the home. The rates are set by the State Board of Insurance in Texas, Florida and New Mexico. In some states like Pennsylvania, Ohio, New York and Delaware, they have bureaus that set the rates. Others do it differently, but the rates are usually the same across the state.

The title company may call you once or twice during your transaction. You will verify information for them concerning marital status, liens, forwarding address, and simple things like this.

In Texas, most transactions are closed at a title company. You will be signing many documents including the deed, the deed of trust and note. The title company will complete the closing statements with the help of the closing department at the mortgage company. The closing department and the title company confer and each reviews all documents. (Note: Whatever the title company attorney does, they are not representing the buyer or the seller. They are simply preparing or reviewing documents to make sure everything is correct and legal.)

If you choose to have your own attorney, they can also prepare documents, like the note, the deed and the deed of trust in certain situations. Every transaction is different.

The closing will take about 30 minutes to one hour for the buyer to sign all the legal documents and provide the **good funds** to close. Good funds consist of the down payment and buyer closing costs usually in the form of a cashier's check. The money can also be wired into the title company's account prior to closing. This is much more convenient and saves time.

Wiring money to a title company is very convenient. The title company must know when they are receiving the funds. **Never send funds from**

information received by email. Talk to the title company personally. Fraud does happen.

When I sold real estate, title company staff would often come to talk with my company during business meetings. The number one fraud they experienced was fraudulent emails sent to buyers or sellers during a transaction. Hackers can get information and send emails that look authentic. Personal conversations will prevent this kind of crime from happening to you.

In other states, closings can take place in realtor® offices, banks, or attorney offices. Mobile notaries are becoming more prominent in use during the covid-19 pandemic. With the new technology that is available, more and more business transactions are being done electronically.

At closing, a photo identification card and driver's license is needed. Many of the papers will be notarized. A copy of everything signed will be given to you. You will get the keys to your new home if possession is given at closing. If the seller keeps possession for a few days, you may have to return to the title company or real estate office to retreive keys when the seller is finished moving out.

You may receive warranty papers at closing for the appliances or systems in the home. These should be put in a secure place for safe keeping.

If you have questions at closing, be sure to ask them. This is the time for having your last minute questions answered. If closing takes longer because of the questions, so be it. Ask the questions and get answers now.

When you sign the final papers and the deed is delivered, you are the home owner. Your homeowners' insurance policy should go into effect this day. Your home is now covered for any losses.

I have seen losses occur on closing day. It gets complicated but it does happen. Make sure you are covered (insured) before you walk out of the title company office.

The deed says the property has been transferred from the seller to you. The deed of trust is a document that says the deed has a lien on it. The deed of trust gives the loan company the authority to take your house if you breach the contract by failing to pay your mortgage payments. The deed and the deed of trust are filed at the courthouse as a public record.

The note is the agreement between you and the loan company. All the terms of the note are designated, such as amount borrowed, interest rate, and number of payments. The note will be held by the mortgage company. You will receive the paid in full note when all payments have been made.

Some mortgage companies "service" their loans. This means they hold those loans for as long as you are making payments. Some companies sell their notes on the open market. This means you could make a loan with a certain company and a few months later, they could sell that note. If they do, you will be informed where you need to make your payments in the future. Do not be concerned, this is very common.

A copy of the filed documents will be mailed to you, but you will walk out of closing with an unfiled copy as well. A copy of your homeowner's insurance policy will be included in your packet. Also a copy of your home warranty and title policy is in your paperwork. There may be many more items. Keep these in a secure place.

Keeping your title policy is a good idea even many years after you sell your home and buy another. Your title policy is good forever. Years in the future, the title could be disputed in a lawsuit. This is your insurance for selling a home with a clear title. This may be something that never comes up. Just keep all your papers until you sell sometime in the future, and always keep the title policy.

Chapter 14

Moving

When moving day comes, there are a thousand items on your list that have already been completed. The utilities have been changed into your name and the turn on date is scheduled. If the home needed repairs, those should have been completed prior to closing. Cleaning of the house and carpets is done and you can move into a clean environment if you have scheduled all these things in advance.

Moving day can occur on closing day but not always. It depends if your home is vacant or the sellers have to move out first. Moving day was established a long time ago when you first contracted to buy your home. The date of possession is in your contract.

Moving requires planning if you want to do it easily. First, pack up the things that are not used on a daily basis. You will have 30-60-90 days during the time your loan is being completed to pack. Pack and store the things you can live without for a short period of time. Be sure to label every box. This is so important.

Put your important papers in a place where you can get to them easily. You may have to produce documents several times during the loan process. I have known people who packed up papers and forgot to label the boxes. Finding a particular document became a nightmare. Be sure and label boxes and put important papers in a place where you can easily access them.

Before the big day comes, you should have researched banks, schools, doctors and utility companies. Know where each is located and what documents they will require for your move.

Research moving companies, get quotes and decide how you will move your furnishings. There are lots of options today from full service moving companies to do-it-yourself trucks you can rent. With so many moving companies and options available, it makes the job easier. You will need to schedule the move in advance as the companies work on tight schedules.

Moving boxes can be purchased at your local home improvement stores or moving companies. Dollies and moving blankets can also be rented. Friends or family can be a big help and may save you some money, if you are fortunate enough to have people help you move.

Make a list of companies you will need to contact for a change of address. Do not forget the accounts online. Changing your address immediately will save any inconvenience caused by mail interruption. You may put in your change of address at the post office many days before you move. Before doing this, make sure your loan has been approved.

Moving is a good time to rid yourself of items you rarely use or need. Donating clothes, furniture, kitchen items, tools, and electronics is a good way to cut some moving expense. It is a great time to clean out the closets.

If you have valuables like jewelry, guns, paperwork or collections, you may want to move these items separately in your own vehicle. Making sure nothing gets lost, stolen, or broken, this is the measurement of success in moving.

It is a good idea to backup your computers before packing them up. Pack a suitcase also, just in case you need some clothes before you get everything unpacked in the new house. Take your medicines with you. Have some cash available for things you may need before you get things set up in the new residence. Be sure to tip your movers.

Moving day is fun and exciting, but everyone in the family will feel some anxiety. Remember, children may experience the most anxiety and not be able to tell you. Give everyone a little space and a little forgiveness if things get overheated. It is hard to leave one place where memories were made, and go to a new place where everything feels uncertain.

You may be second guessing yourself, asking "Did I do the right thing?"

Take a deep breath and just be happy. You have come a long way from dreaming to reality, and you did it! You accomplished your goal. Your hard work paid off. Now, enjoy your reward. Your new home will be the place where new memories are made. This time you won't have to leave because the rent was raised or the property sold to a new owner. This home is yours!

Chapter 15

Maintenance and Landscaping

Most books about buying your new home stop at the closing table. This is not the end of the story, but only the beginning. New home owners rarely know much about maintenance, but it is important to learn. Maintaining your home in good condition will ensure you get top dollar if you ever want to sell it. It will also add enjoyment to your property if you keep everything in working order.

If you were fortunate to get a home warranty with your purchase, you can rest assured things will be taken care of if they break within the first year.

After the year is up, you may renew this coverage if you so desire. People often carry home warranties for years. It is easier when you have someone to call and you know the warranty will cover the cost. Your warranty is actually an insurance policy insuring the systems in your home.

Apart from a separate home warranty, did your homeowner's insurance agent tell you about extended home coverage your company also offers? This is available on most policies now for a minimal fee. Be sure to ask. It is just additional coverage. It rarely covers as much as a separate home warranty, but comes in handy in case you need it. If you have a problem, you may be paid twice.

When warranties do not come into play, there may be some things you will need to take care of personally. The biggest threat to your home is water intrusion. Make sure there are no leaks and if one develops, hopefully there is a water valve close by to turn off. This will prevent water damage from occurring until you get someone to fix the leak. Know where your water valves are located before you need to find them. If you decide to fix a water leak, make sure you know what you are doing. Your home improvement stores have books on home maintenance, and I suggest first-time home buyers get one and read how to take care of minor maintenance issues.

Keeping all the wood on your home painted or stained will keep the wood from rotting. I have seen so many homes where the wood on the facia or eaves was rotten. This must be replaced before selling a home. It also says the homeowner did not keep the wood painted or stained. What other things did they not take care of, is the question potential buyers will be asking.

You need to change the filters on your air conditioning/heating unit on a regular basis. Buy a supply of filters and mark the date on the top of the filter when you change it out. I like to change mine on the first day of each month that I change them. This is an easy way not to forget. Keeping your filters clean will not only give you cleaner air to breathe in your home, but extend the life of your unit and save you money on repair bills.

There are differences in the filters you buy. Some are only good for one month. Some will last for 3 months. I suggest the better ones as their performance will filter your air better. The extra cost for better air filters is returned with fewer maintenance bills from your air conditioning/heating unit.

As a Realtor®, when I walk into a room and see the air duct in the ceiling and there is dirt around it, I immediately know there could be maintenance issues. I know the owner has not been changing the filters regularly. It can say a lot about neglected home maintenance.

Bathtubs often need caulking to keep water from getting behind walls and ruining sheetrock. This is a simple job anyone can do, but it is so important. Check caulking around sinks as well. If you do not take care of this problem, mold could grow behind the sheetrock. This would be a very expensive repair. Mold is dangerous. It can cause severe illness. Take care of the problem before it happens.

There are many things you can do to keep your home looking nice, and **regular maintenance costs much less than repairs.** Buy a book and learn how to do these simple jobs. A small toolbox, some paintbrushes, and simple tools can save you lots of money. Your home is your biggest single investment, so maintain its value by maintaining the home.

Landscaping is something that adds curb appeal, but not always a monetary value to your home. Landscaping is important for your families' enjoyment. Trees, grass, bushes, flowers, rock gardens, fountains, gazebos, patios and pathways give your home that special touch. Your landscaping says a lot about who lives in the house. It is a way to enjoy nature and to showcase your decorating prowess if you so desire.

I have always told my sellers before I listed a home for sale, their landscaping may sell the home, but it will not increase the appraised value very much. So, keep this in mind when you are planning big projects outside. If you are doing the project for yourself, spend as much as you want. But if you are doing it to increase the value, think again. Ask your Realtor® to do a CMA to determine how much value your project will add. Plan ahead, but enjoy your new home. Make the outside as lovely as the inside.

Do not plant trees close to the house. Roots can be a problem for foundations and plumbing. They can also damage your home if the wind blows them onto your roof in years to come when they are fully grown. Plan ahead carefully.

Bushes and flowerbeds near the foundation will keep your foundation moist when you water them. If you have a cement slab foundation and live in the South where it is hot and dry, this will help keep your foundation from cracking.

I advise my clients in the South, to water the foundation once or twice a month during the summer because of highly expansive clay soil. If you have flowerbeds, you only need to water the areas that are not getting regular moisture.

People who live in the North rarely have problems like dry foundations. Instead, they worry about water intrusion in basements. There are products to seal basement floors and walls. It is fairly easy to apply and will save you money if it has not been done in the past.

A freshly mowed grassy yard is so nice to look at, and for children and pets to play ball. There are many varieties of grass available. Check with the local nursery or extension agent to find out which kind is best for your area before spending a lot of money installing a new yard. If you live in a hot and dry climate, be sure to buy a drought resistant variety. Water bills can be extreme in the south. But water is necessary to protect and grow the grass.

Gravel yards are becoming more popular in sunny locations. They are more expensive to install but less work, less maintenance, and less expensive over time. Some people prefer them instead of grass and use more bushes and flowers to accent their landscaping.

Landscaping is a matter of taste and preference. If the outdoor space is maintained well, the home has more curb appeal and will sell quickly when you decide to sell. It's your home, make it yours with the plants you love.

One thing new home owners should have is an emergency fund. There is no stress if you have money saved for emergencies like a water heater replacement, or money for the deductible on your insurance from a hailstorm. Things happen and emergencies occur when you least expect it. If you have money saved for such things, it makes life so much easier. Plan ahead and put some money aside for home maintenance.

Many financial experts stress the importance of an emergency fund in their books on personal finance. They say an emergency fund is essential, suggesting a three to six month emergency fund in case you lose your job. This money is used for living expenses and other emergencies. I suggest having an emergency fund available for every first-time homeowner.

Until you can build your emergency fund, find $500–$2,000 and put that away. I am suggesting a special amount tucked away just for unexpected home maintenance. Put some money in the cookie jar for this and you will rest easy at night.

Home ownership is a big responsibility you have never experienced before. It may frighten you, but knowing all that is required makes it less scary. Owning your own home is like being in charge of your destiny. Controlling where and how you live brings confidence and peace of mind.

Chapter 16

Real Life Experiences of First-Time Homebuyers

I remember the day I got the call from Denita. Her voice shook as she explained her predicament. Denita was divorced and she had a child. Her ex-husband was threatening to take her to court for custody of their child.

Denita was scared. She worked at a restaurant and the money was good enough but the record keeping was lacking. She had a parttime job cleaning houses on the side to make extra money.

We talked for a few minutes and she said she did not know why she called me. She saw my sign in front of my office and it was a whim. I told her, "No, it's not a problem. Why don't you come in and let's talk?"

She was hesitant at first but recanted and we made an appointment to meet. When she came in, she appeared anxious and after a cup of coffee and chatting, I began to ask pertinent questions.

"Why do you want to own a home?"

She felt her child would be happier and more settled if she owned rather than rented their home. Denita had experienced several moves in the past two years and she knew she and her child suffered from the instability. She felt her ex-husband would have less of a chance in court if she was a homeowner. During the recent moves, her child had also moved schools. So, being in one place with one school was an important aspect of Denita's desire to own.

At this point, I understood Denita's motivation. This is the most important thing for any Realtor® to know. I wanted to help her. My heart ached for her. She was so sincere and was trying so hard to make life good for her child.

Once we developed trust and she agreed to allow me to help her, we began to explore the possibilities of a loan. With a job that did not have steady income week to week, it was a challenge. Waitresses get paid very little for hourly work. Most of their wages come in tips. Tips are not steady and can vary from week to week and month to month.

Denita had another parttime job. This added to her income stream but it was parttime and temporary.

Denita made enough money to afford a reasonably priced home. I gave her the name of a loan originator I used often. He ran her credit report and attempted to pre-qualify her for a loan. Her credit was fair. She had several late pays and one bad mark. I knew it would take a while to fix these things.

The loan originator told her what she had to do. It would take a couple months to repair these items but it could be done. Denita was happy and a little surprised. She now had hope of becoming a homeowner. It was a big deal. She was 30 years old and had never owned a home or property. She could now dream of homeownership and know it was a real possibility. The first thing she had to do was get her credit report in good shape.

I called Denita once a week for a couple of months. We developed a good friendship during this time. She brought her credit scores up where she needed to be. Now, we would call her loan originator and let him check her credit report again. If it showed a high enough credit score, we would go to the next step.

It did. Denita was thrilled, she had brought her score up 38 points and now she was in the qualifying range. The loan originator asked her to bring him her w-2's from the past two years and her income tax returns. She did. Her income was not steady. Some months were down and some were up. The tips were counted differently from time to time. Her parttime job sometimes earned more than the fulltime job but it was not steady income.

The loan originator told her she would not be approved for a loan with unsteady income streams. She was heartbroken. I was disappointed too but I told her there might be another way. I knew an independent lender in a nearby town. If she wanted to go that way, he might consider a loan for her. The interest rate charged is always more with an independent investor like this. That is the downside. What else could Denita do?

We made an appointment. Denita was happy with the opportunity presented to her. Now, we knew she could get a loan and what price range she would qualify for. We began to look for homes.

There was nothing on the market that suited her, or met her needs. I told her she must be patient, something will come along. One week later, a new listing popped up and we made the first appointment to look at the home. Denita loved it. It was perfect. It was the right size, in the right location and the school bus ran right outside the door. The yard was fenced and it was a little below her price range.

We went to the office and wrote a purchase offer. I presented it to the listing agent that day. Later in the evening, the agent called me to say there were a few things that had to be negotiated. She also said there was another offer that had been presented later that day.

I met with Denita and discussed the negotiating points and we made our counter. Denita knew we took a chance of losing the home if we did not accept the sellers' conditions but she was firm with what she needed. We held our breath to hear what the seller was going to do. We did not know until the following afternoon. I am sure they were considering the other offer as well.

They took Denita's offer. We escrowed the contract and Denita gave the earnest money to the title company. Now, it was my job to send the contract to the lender and I made appointments for Denita's home inspectors.

After a week, the home was inspected and approved by Denita and her loan was being worked. She was approved for the loan and we closed the transaction within a month. Denita got the keys to her new home and began moving in. She changed the door locks first thing.

A week later, she was all moved in. I was invited to dinner.

Denita was a hard-working single mother who never believed she could become a homeowner. She took the chance and followed good advice from her Realtor® and loan originator. She followed through and did the work of repairing her credit and it paid off. The first loan originator did not make the loan and did not get paid for his service since he worked on commission but he helped her anyway. There are many loan originators and some will go out of their way to help people.

If you are in Denita's shoes, know it can be done. Dreams do come true.

*****

Another real life story is about Jon and Mandy. I met them when they called about a rental I had listed. They were too late, it had just rented that day. I started talking to them about what they needed and asked if they had considered buying instead of renting.

Jon & Mandy had been living together for a year but were not married yet. They planned to marry in the future but they were waiting for now. They had not considered buying but Jon's salary as a city employee was steady and his job secure. Mandy had just started working for Wal-Mart. They had not developed much credit, but like I always say, "no credit is better than bad credit."

We looked at a couple of homes that might have been in their price range and I was able to show them the difference in buying versus renting. The difference in that area at that time was significant. They could buy a bigger and better home for the same money they could rent one for. The decision was made to get pre-approved for a loan if possible.

Once again, the loan approval was difficult but with a good loan originator working very hard for Jon and Mandy, it became a reality. It took a total of 4 ½ months from start to finish but they were determined to make it happen. Sometimes, it takes longer than usual. Sometimes, there are many hoops you must jump through. The successful people do what is needed to make it happen.

Today, Jon and Mandy are living comfortably in that home. They married a year after they bought and I was invited to their wedding. Then a few years later, they became the proud parents of two beautiful children. I have remained friends with them all this time. Working with them was such a pleasure. I love seeing people's dreams come true.

*****

Lisa called my office one Autumn day. Her grandfather had recently passed and he willed her some money. She had considered many different ways of investing the money but decided it would be best if she bought a home. Lisa was single, employed fulltime, and had a busy social calendar.

She told me she needed a nice place where she could have some peaceful, quiet time. She said her life was very busy, but sometimes she just wanted to relax with a good book. Lisa wanted her new home to be a sanctuary with some pretty plants and trees on her patio. She wanted a special place, not hurried like her life.

I did some research and came up with the perfect place. It was a condo on the golf course. The patio was totally enclosed with large limestone blocks. There were trees, flowering bushes, and even a small fountain in the corner. Large enough for a few friends, but cozy enough for Lisa on her chaise lounge reading her favorite novel. Loveliness, peacefulness, and a condo with landscaping provided weekly by the association. It was perfect.

This transaction only took a matter of weeks to close. Lisa's credit was good, she had the down payment and closing costs, and had found the perfect place quickly. Buying your first home, can be quick or it can take some time. Every transaction is different.

Do not have pre-conceived ideas. Let your Realtor® and your loan originator help you. There are also ways to finance a home other than the traditional mortgage. Your seasoned Realtor® will know of ways to help you, such as owner financing or independent investors like Denita used. Remember the old saying, **"Where there's a will, there's a way."**

*****

Trevor came into my office on a Friday afternoon. He had a three day weekend. He also had a plan. He was active military, stationed in a nearby city and had never bought a home before. He was single but wanted to eventually have a family but this was not his reason for buying. He wanted to begin to build equity in a home and eventually own many homes and rent them out as a retirement source of income.

Trevor could use a VA loan and buy a home with zero down payment. My town was not far from his military base and he could easily drive it every day. He could live in the home while stationed in the area and rent it out when he was transferred. He asked if I could manage his property in the future. Of course, I said yes!

Trevor had a good clean credit report and his loan processed quickly. He decided to buy in this area because it was a steady market with high resale figures in case he decided to sell in the future. It was not his plan, however. He wanted to keep the home permanently and use it as rental property if he was stationed elsewhere.

Trevor was a smart man and he lived in the home for a year and half before being transferred. He wanted to rent the home when he left the area. I leased the home for a year at a time to military families and managed the property while he was away. Surprisingly, he was restationed nearby about five years later and moved back into the home. At that time, he had bought two other properties in different cities. His retirement plan was on track.

*****

I have sold to many first-time home buyers but Candice was one of the more interesting transactions I had. I want to share two important things about this one. First of all, she was single with 2 small children. She was renting a single family home but wanted a place of her own. She wanted her rental money going into a home she owned herself. She had a good job and a fair credit rating.

She called me after she had looked in the area she wanted to live. She found a home that was listed with a discount broker. This discount broker did not work well with other brokers in our area and did not use our MLS. They were not subject to MLS rules. Red flag!

She was sold on this house. She wanted me to go look at it and write a contract for her. I went to view the property. As I walked up the driveway, I could see a huge crack on the outside brick veneer wall. It went from the top of the wall to the bottom of the wall. I was astounded that someone would not have repaired this and I knew it could mean serious foundation issues.

The home had been vacant for a while and it smelled of mold. The kitchen needed a complete overhaul. The walls would need painting, and the floors needed new floor covering. As I inspected it further, the master bathroom had water penetration from several areas. There was mold.

This was not the house for a single Mom that worked fulltime. She had no experience doing remodeling and nobody to help her do the repairs that would be needed. She had no idea how much a remodel like this would cost. I gave her a quick estimate and that was without the foundation issues. I had to completely educate Candice on home construction before she could understand this was a losing siutation that would leave her exhausted and broke. It was not a good deal.

You may find a foreclosure that looks like a bargain because of a low price. When you count the cost of the remodel, it may not be a bargain at all. You must count the cost of materials, labor, and your time and energy as well. Foreclosures often are not maintained well by previous owners. Deferred maintenance can be costly. Most of the time, foreclosures are not a wise choice for first-time home buyers because most have no knowledge of construction or home maintainance. A home that the seller has lived in and maintained regularly is a better buy even at a more expensive price.

The second thing Candice's transaction had that I think is worth mentioning to first-time home buyers concerned the closing. Candice was buying a home that was vacant. The home belonged to a man that was living in a foreign country and this had not been revealed.

Candice was anxious to move into her new home. As soon as her loan was approved, we started planning to close. The seller was not able to close on time. He was out of the country and in an area where there was no communication. He would not be in an area with internet for more than two weeks. Candice needed to move, her landlord had already leased her place to someone else. There was a time crunch. What could we do?

Candice leased the home for 2 weeks before it closed. This is called a Buyer's Temporary Lease. She had to make a security deposit like a regular lease. She had to pay for two weeks rent. She also had to buy two weeks of renter's insurance until she closed. It was a hassle and it cost a lot of money to do this. She had no other choice unless she wanted to back out. It had already been 3 months finding a house and getting her loan approved.

It was stressful but when she finally closed, it was a very happy day with lots of photos and celebrations. Today, she would tell you it was worth the effort. She has made a wonderful home for herself and her children.

Buyer's Temporary Leases and Seller's Temporary Leases are used whenever situations like this occur. When buyers need to move in before closing, or sellers need to stay for a short time after closing, we use a lease like this to protect everyone.

Glossary of Terms

Abstract of title is a collection of documents showing legal transactions concerning the subject property. It may go back to the beginning of the country. An abstract will not guarantee the title is good. It just shows the lists of transactions that have occurred. Sometimes, the list may be missing transactions that could put a cloud, which is an encumbrance, on the title. In this case, the title policy which is an insurance policy, will protect the new buyer from a lawsuit that could arise from a previous owner's family that claims ownership in your property.

Amortization is paying payments of principal and interest regularly until the amount of money owed is paid in full.

Appraisal is a written report prepared by a qualified and unbiased appraiser as to the current fair market value of a property. The value is determined by comparison of other similar properties that have recently sold in the same area. Mortgage companies require appraisals to determine the value of a property in which they may loan money for purchase.

Attorney is the only person who can give legal advice. You may want an attorney to look at a contract before signing it. You may want your attorney to also look at closing documents before signing them. The title company will prepare some of the documents and attornies that work for the title company will prepare the deed and deed of trust and other documents. These attornies will make sure the documents are prepared correctly but they do not work directly for you. They do not represent you in the transaction. You may hire an attorney that represents you to look at all documents if you wish.

Buyer's Estimated Costs will detail costs of loan application, appraisal fees, attorney fees, proration of taxes and insurance, survey, recording of deed, courier, interest and many other things. You will be aware of some of these expenses from the estimate your mortgage lender has given you. This will be more detailed because now you have a specific house in mind. Your Realtor® will provide this.

Buyer's Rep Agreement is an agreement between the buyer and the real estate agent. The buyer agrees to hire the agent to represent them in the real estate transaction. Fees are often paid by the seller.

Cloud is a claim or encumbrance, such as a lien that impairs the right to transfer ownership.

CMA, Comparative Market Analysis is similar to an appraisal. A real estate agent will provide buyers and sellers with a CMA to help them determine a selling price. The agent is not authorized to do an appraisal, only licensed appraisers can do this. The CMA is a comparison of recently sold homes in an area but is not as thorough as an appraisal. Agents get their information from multiple listing services.

Contract in real estate terms is a legally binding, written, dated document where two parties agree upon price and terms to sell/buy with their signatures affixed with a stated date for completion of contract and transferance of property. It will be the complete agreement between the parties and will include ALL parts of the agreement. It could be 15-30 pages long.

Deed is the document that conveys real property from seller to buyer.

Down Payment is the amount of money required to pay at the time of closing. It is subtracted from the purchase price of the home to find the loan amount.

Earnest money is an amount usually ranging from 1-5% of the purchase price of the home, held by the title company as good faith money. It tells the seller you are serious about buying their house. They will take their house off the market while you obtain your loan to purchase. The earnest money is applied to down payment and fees you will owe at closing. If you back out of the contract **for no reason**, the seller will get to keep your earnest money.

Escrowed contract is one where all parties have signed and now it is taken to the title company and date stamped. Buyers and sellers are given a copy for their records. The option period begins. The title company is given the earnest money to hold until closing when it is applied to the buyer's costs.

Escrow account is an account held by the mortgage company for you. The account is set up at closing, with money paid by you, for taxes and insurance when they become due and payable. The mortgage company will pay these costs automatically every year.

HUD Statement or closing statement will detail all expenses you will pay at the completion of your transaction. This is like the buyer's estimated costs but it is not an estimate. It is the actual costs, and these costs are accurate to the day of closing, such as daily interest and pro-ration of taxes.

Insurance is a homeowner's insurance policy which will insure your home against damage caused by various things such as fire and wind damage. Included in homeowner's insurance is insurance for contents, your personal belongings. This is an additional 40% of the amount of coverage you have on your home. You may need flood insurance or windstorm insurance as well. We discuss this thoroughly in chapter 11.

Interest is an amount of money paid over the amount borrowed. It is figured as a percentage. Most current mortgage rates are between 3% and 4%. These are historically low rates, making it a good time to buy. The rates can change quickly with the market. Over the past 40 years, I have seen the rates change dramatically from a low 3% currently to 20% in the early 1980's. Lower rates mean you can afford a more expensive home than if the rates were higher.

Mineral Rights are conveyed at closing depending on what the contract says. Mineral rights may be retained by the seller. The seller may own the mineral rights or not. Those rights could belong to someone else who owned the property in previous years.

MIP is the government mortgage insurance policy for FHA loans. It is designed to reduce the risk of borrowers defaulting on their loans.

PITI A portion of your monthly house payment goes for each of these: Principal, Interest, Taxes, and Insurance. The monthly house payment is called PITI.

PMI is private mortgage insurance. It is similar to MIP used for government loans but PMI is for private mortgage companies. Both MIP and PMI provide insurance for the lender in case the borrower defaults.

Principal is the amount borrowed, the price of your home minus the down payment. It is divided into monthly payments. It is amortized with the interest payment to find the monthly amount due.

Property Taxes are taxes you must pay based on the assessed value of your property and any improvements to the land (basically your home, garage, and out buildings). You will pay taxes to the city, the county, the school district, the township, hospital district, maybe water district, and other entities in your area. It will generally be billed to you in one statement once or twice a year depending on your state, county or township. These will automatically be paid if they are included in an escrow account attached to your monthly house payment.

Purchase Agreement is the same thing as an offer to buy. It contains all the same things a contract contains but has not been approved by the seller. An offer may be returned to the buyer as rejected, approved, or some details may be changed. All revisions must be approved by the buyer. Changes can be made several times before both buyer and seller completely agree to the price and terms. All revisions should be made in writing and the appropriate Amendment to Contract forms should be used.

Real Property is land and any structure that is attached to the land like buildings or houses. It includes crops, mineral rights, water rights, everything under the land and above the land to a degree. Air space rights are complicated.

Restrictions known as deed restrictions, covenants, and restrictive covenants are contained in the deed and state how you can use the property. These restrictions are usually placed on the property at the time it is developed and continue with each conveyance. HOA's also place restrictions on property. Get a copy of the restrictive covenants as soon as possible and read them before you buy. Make sure you agree with all restricitons. They cannot be changed.

Seller's Disclosure Notice is an ackowledgment by the seller of anything that is wrong with the house you are considering. It should include any repairs made in recent years or inspection reports. It will include many things from defects to boundary or insurance disputes. You should read it carefully. It is a legal document.

Single family home is self explanatory. It is a one unit home in a neighborhood of similar properties.

Subdivision is a parcel of land divided into smaller tracts of land, or lots with streets, utilities, and restrictions. Once developed, it will contain a number of homes and become a neighborhood.

Survey is a drawing of the property with boundary lines marked. It will show where buildings are located and provide dimensions of buildings and land. You must have a survey to show no buildings or fences are encroaching upon another parcel or are located in the lot setback areas. Surveys are certified by a registered surveyor.

Title policy is an insurance policy a title company issues to insure the title is good. It guarantees there are no clouds on the title. Everyone should get a title policy or abstract when they purchase property. A title policy is always good and you should keep it even after you sell the property. In case there is ever a dispute about ownership, it has a monetary value to you if you are involved in a lawsuit to prove ownership.

Termination of Contract can be given to the seller if the buyer does not approve of the property after the inspections are made. This must be done before the option period lapses. Or, if the buyer cannot obtain a loan before the loan approval date in the contract, the buyer may also give a termination of contract to seller and may receive a return of earnest money. Time is of the essence in all contracts and you must abide by the dates written in the contract.

Water rights are not applicable in urban areas but in rural areas they are very important. Your contract should address these if applicable.

Zoning laws or restrictions allow for certain uses to your real property. Know the zoning laws before you purchase.

Author Notes

I want to thank you for reading this book. I hope you have gleaned a lot of information that will help you buy your first home. I remember the thrill of buying my first home. That feeling was like no other.

I hope this will be the beginning of a real estate journey that brings happiness and security to you. The American Dream of home ownership is what many people have dreamed for decades. We are privileged in this country to have the opportunity to buy land, and properties that become our homes. A place where memories are made and shared by our loved ones.

The real estate industry has gone through many changes in the past few years. The pandemic brought uncertainty, along with the disease that killed many people and upended careers and jobs for many others.

The market in 2020 and 2021 was so hot first-time homebuyers had little chance of buying a home.

There were multiple offers on most listings as soon as they hit the market. It was unbelievable what happened.

It was not just first-time homebuyers acting out of fear of never being able to buy if they did not buy then. It was large corporations buying up single family homes to rent out to desperate want-to-be-homeowners. Greed was pushing the cost of homes upward.

Before the rush was over, the average cost of a home had increased to the point of pricing most first-time buyers out of the market. Then, the interest rates began increasing. They leveled off at about seven percent. The unheard-of rates of two and a half or three percent were gone. So, was the opportunity to buy.

It normally takes years for interest rates to change drastically. However, we are not living in normal times. Nobody knows what will happen until it does. Experts can predict, but they are not always right.

Removing fraud, waste, and abuse from our government will help with inflation. When our economy gets to running better, we will most likely see the mortgage interest rates go down. This will help first-time homebuyers to afford to buy a home. Our country still needs to build more housing. This would drop the cost and allow even more people to own their homes.

We will see changes. Watch the national market, and also watch your local market. They are not always in sync. Watch for an opportunity to buy. The cost of a home, plus the interest rate you will have to pay will determine if it is a good time for you. Be prepared to act fast. Preparation is the key to a good deal. Being ready when the opportunity affords itself is what a wise person does.

We have wonderful privileges in this country to own real estate. This privilege is not shared in every country in the world. We are blessed with Private Property Rights. Learn about them and defend them always.

Happy Home Hunting, First-Time Home Buyers!

If you have enjoyed this book, please go to www.Amazon.com/author/rickimccallum and give me a review. It would be greatly appreciated.

Sign up for my free weekly blog at www.castnetpress.com Find all kinds of information on real estate, home maintenance, market trends, etc.

www.ingramcontent.com/pod-product-compliance
Lightning Source LLC
Chambersburg PA
CBHW070636220526
45466CB00001B/189